SECRETS, LIES, GIZMOS, AND SPIES

A History of Spies and Espionage

BY **JANET WYMAN COLEMAN**

WITH THE **INTERNATIONAL SPY MUSEUM**

ABRAMS BOOKS FOR YOUNG READERS
NEW YORK

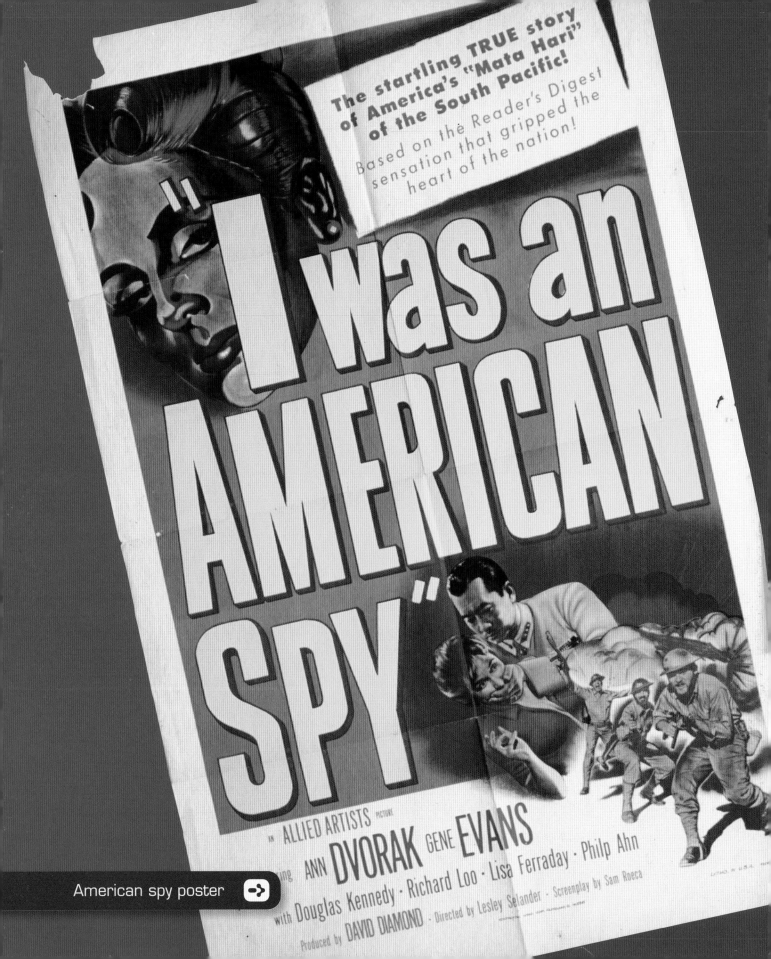
American spy poster

SO YOU'RE INTERESTED IN SPIES...

IN THIS BOOK, you will read about believable and unbelievable spies, impressive weapons, classified operations, and artful deceptions. You can't learn everything about espionage, because spies and intelligence agencies keep many secrets. The names and successes of some of the bravest men and women will never be revealed, but they're out there, listening, learning, lying—alive and dead.

Perhaps you're interested in the CIA, the FBI, or intelligence agencies around the world. (There are hundreds.) Or do heroes and villains fascinate you? Spies can be both. They steal secrets to help one side but, at the same time, sabotage another. Hero, villain, or traitor? It depends which side you're on.

Imagine risking your life for what you believe in. Many spies can't tell their families what they do, where they're going, or when they'll return. Of course, some people steal secrets for money or diamonds, but many risk their lives because they believe in one way of life or another. In the process, they can change history.

In the interest of full disclosure, I'll warn you that this book isn't predictable. Spies aren't predictable. *Secrets, Lies, Gizmos, and Spies* isn't a complete history of spying from the beginning until this very moment. Instead, it's a collection of spy stories organized by what they have in common. For example, what's the connection between the Trojan Horse (1200 BCE) and The Thing (1946 CE)? Confused? Don't give up. Sooner or later, the pieces will fall into place.

TELLING a friend may mean telling THE ENEMY

American spy poster

> The [intelligence] game is akin to putting a puzzle together without all the pieces, or a box top to guide you, and with several parts of other puzzles thrown in.
>
> —*Martin Petersen,* CIA analyst

KEY TERMS

Abwehr: Germany's military intelligence organization during the 1930s and early 1940s. It established the largest spy ring ever to operate in the United States (as far as we know).

Cheka: The Soviet agency responsible for state security (1917–1922). This agency evolved into many others over the years and, in 1954, became the KGB.

CIA: The U.S. Central Intelligence Agency, created in 1947. The CIA uses intelligence, counterintelligence, and covert action for national security. The intelligence comes from spies working for the U.S., as well as from sophisticated technology. Counterintelligence focuses on enemy spies. The head of the CIA reports to the director of national intelligence.

Cold War: The competition between the United States and its allies and the Soviet Union and its allies that began at the end of the World War II (approximately) and ended with the collapse of the Soviet Union in 1991.

DNI: Director of National Intelligence, a post created in 2004.

FELIKS DZERZHINSKY
"We stand for organized terror," said Dzerzhinsky, the founder of the Cheka. The ruthless leader used spy craft against his own citizens and oversaw the deaths of more than two hundred thousand suspected counter-revolutionaries.

WILLIAM DONOVAN
"Wild Bill" Donovan was the director of the OSS. Donovan urged President Roosevelt to create a permanent foreign intelligence agency. After President Roosevelt died, President Truman disbanded the OSS. Two years later, Truman established the CIA.

FAPSI: Russian counterpart to the U.S. NSA (National Security Agency). The Soviet "federal agency of governmental communication" was formed in 1991.

FBI: The U.S. Federal Bureau of Investigation, created in 1935, is a descendant of the BI, the Bureau of Investigation. The FBI seeks to protect the U.S. from foreign intelligence operations, espionage, and terrorist attacks. It also combats domestic crime (public corruption, white-collar crime, violent crime, criminal organizations) and protects civil rights.

Gestapo: Nazi Germany's Secret Police (1933–1945).

GRU: (1918–today) Soviet/Russian military intelligence agency created under Lenin.

HVA: East German foreign intelligence, part of the Stasi.

Jedburgh: An elite team of British and American intelligence officers and radiomen trained by the SOE and OSS. The teams worked with members of the French Resistance during World War II. Ninety-three Jedburgh teams parachuted into France after the Normandy invasion. (Jedburgh is the Scottish city where the "Jedburghs" trained.)

In the early years of the FBI, agents who hunted down gangsters were called G-men.

KGB: The Soviet agency responsible for foreign intelligence and domestic security (1954–1991). The KGB was probably larger than all Western intelligence agencies combined.

Maquis: An organization formed by French communists and socialists, part of the French Resistance during World War II. Members were called Maquisards.

MI5: The British domestic counterintelligence service. It is focused on internal security within the United Kingdom. (MI stands for military intelligence.)

MI6: The British foreign intelligence service. It conducts operations to obtain intelligence and disrupts threats from foreign sources. It is also known as SIS.

NSA: The National Security Agency, which includes the Central Security Service (CSS). The NSA protects U.S. information systems and produces foreign intelligence by intercepting and decoding foreign communications. It is the principal American code-breaking organization.

OSS: The Office of Strategic Services, the American foreign intelligence service during World War II. It was modeled in part on the British SOE. More than seventeen thousand men and four thousand women worked for the OSS during the war. They sabotaged the Nazis and Japanese throughout Europe and Asia, and generated thousands of intelligence leads—OB (order of battle) information about enemy strength, deployment, weapons, morale, etc. (The OSS was disbanded in 1945.)

Pentagon: The five-sided building that is the headquarters of the Department of Defense in Washington, D.C. "The Pentagon" is often used to refer to the leaders of the U.S. military.

SIS: The British Secret Intelligence Service, established in 1909. It is also known as MI6.

SOE: British Special Operations Executive. It was established in 1940 to engage in "sabotage, subversion, and the formation of resistance groups in German-occupied Europe." Winston Churchill instructed the SOE to "set Europe ablaze!"

Soviet Union, USSR: The Soviet Union or Union of Soviet Socialist Republics was the name of all the Soviet states or republics from 1922 to 1991. The largest was Russia, so the country was commonly called Russia, and the people Russians. (The only political party was the Communist Party of the Soviet Union.) When the USSR dissolved, the post-Soviet states or former Soviet republics became independent nations. Today, Russia refers to just one former Soviet republic.

Stasi: East Germany's Ministry of State Security. It used more than 90,000 officers and 173,000 informers during the Cold War. (For many years, it was a puppet of the KGB.) The Stasi stored thousands of jars with the scents of suspects, and trained dogs to hunt them down. It was dismantled in 1990.

SVR: Russia's foreign intelligence service, established in 1991. Up until that time, foreign intelligence activities were coordinated by the KGB.

MARKUS WOLF
For thirty years, Markus Wolf directed foreign intelligence for the Stasi. Few people in the West knew his identity until 1978, so he was referred to as "the man without a face."

CLOSE YOUR EYES AND imagine a spy. Is he a tall man in his thirties or forties, wearing an overcoat and black shoes? Or do you see a striking brunette hugging something to her ribs? What is she holding? Documents? Photographs? A weapon?

The men and women of the intelligence services around the world are quite different. Foreign agents in the United States may resemble your history teacher or even your parents. They speak perfect English, but use American slang. Overseas, the intelligence game is played the same way. In London, most spies have a British accent. In Moscow, they're fluent in Russian. Occasionally, a celebrity or well-known businessperson will pass secrets, but the average agent looks, talks, and acts like everyone else.

Who was the first spy? It was probably a man who climbed a tree to find out what his neighbor was doing. With one arm wrapped around the trunk, he peered over the wall. Why were his neighbor's goats so healthy and cheerful? What was he feeding them? Where did he get his food? The goal of the first spy was to gather intelligence.

Sean Connery as James Bond, the classic spy!

The first written record of spying was in 1800 BCE. Officials inspected captured clay tablets in King Hammurabi's palace to learn about their enemies. They kept track of tips from the marketplace, rumors from gossips, and reports from the queen. On one secret tablet, modern cryptographers discovered a death warrant: "If there is a ditch in the countryside or in the city," it says, "make this man disappear."

But the first spy wasn't interested in death warrants, just goats and food. Suppose that he didn't learn anything from his perch high up in the tree. He would have shimmied down the trunk and considered another plan. Perhaps he put on a disguise and slipped behind enemy lines.

TIME LINE

1800 BCE: Carvings on a clay tablet from King Hammurabi's palace represent the first written record of spying.

1200 BCE: A large wooden horse rolls into **Troy.** (p. 66)

500 BCE: *Ping-fa*, **The Art of War**, the earliest known text book on war and espionage, is written by Sun Tzu in China. (p. 6)

1778: Members of the **Culper Spy Ring** relay information about the British to General George Washington. (p. 9)

1778: Benjamin Franklin becomes ambassador to France. He is responsible for diplomacy and foreign intelligence collection. (p. 38)

1861: America's first photojournalist, **Alexander Gardner**, uses his camera to spy for the Union. (p. 23)

1863: Harriet Tubman organizes a network of spies and scouts to slip behind Confederate lines. (p. 100)

1865: The Thirteenth Amendment to the Constitution is ratified, abolishing slavery.

1911: The first photographs are taken from an airplane.

1914–1918: World War I

1915: A fearless British nurse and spy, **Edith Cavell,** is shot by a German firing squad. (p. 101)

1917: Russian Revolution

1919: The carrier pigeon **Cher Ami** dies of war wounds. (p. 26)

1930s–1963: Five well-educated Englishmen spy for the Russians (the **Cambridge spies**). (p. 94)

1939–1945: World War II

196 BCE: The **Rosetta Stone** is carved. (p. 30)

1570: Sir Francis Walsingham, chief advisor to Elizabeth I in England, administers the most powerful spy network of the time. (p. 34)

1587: Mary, Queen of Scots, is beheaded. (p. 34)

1775–1783: Revolutionary War in America

1776: The Continental Congress ratifies the Declaration of Independence.

1798: The Sedition Act criminalizes the publication of anything "false, scandalous, or malicious" against the U.S. government.

1814: The White House, the Capitol, and many important public buildings are torched by the British Army.

1861–1865: Civil War in America

1866: The Ku Klux Klan is founded.

1894: French captain **Alfred Dreyfus** is convicted of treason and sent to Devil's Island. (p. 92)

1908: The Department of Justice establishes the Bureau of Investigation, which would become the FBI in 1935.

1917: The Espionage Act imposes punishment (including death) for any activities that weaken or imperil America's defense in wartime or peace. (Most of the act was repealed in 1948.)

1918: The Sabotage Act makes it a crime to damage property or utilities used in connection with a war. (It was repealed in 1948.)

1940: The Special Operations Executive (SOE) is established by the British.

1940: The Japanese Purple Code is broken at **Arlington Hall.** (p. 40)

1941 (December 7): The Japanese attack **Pearl Harbor**. (p. 90)

1942: Twenty-nine Navajos begin training to become "**code talkers.**" (p. 41)

1942: German saboteurs land in Amagansett, New York, and near Jacksonville, Florida (**Operation Pastorius**). (p. 72)

1942: President Roosevelt establishes the Office of Strategic Services (OSS), a U.S. intelligence and sabotage agency.

1945: Frederick Yeo-Thomas (The White Rabbit) escapes for the last time. (p. 81)

1945: The U.S. drops two nuclear bombs on Japan. The weapons are developed in the top-secret **Manhattan Project**. (p. 78)

1956: Harvey's Hole is discovered (**Operation Stopwatch/Gold**). (p. 69)
1957: The Soviet Union launches the first satellite, *Sputnik 1*. (p. 24)

1958: The U.S. launches its first satellite, *Explorer 1*. (p. 24)
1960: Lt. Francis Gary Power's U-2 spy plane is shot down. He is captured by the Russians. (p. 29)

1967: John Walker walks into the Soviet Embassy in Washington, D.C., and announces that he has secrets to sell. (p. 20)

1981: Operation Ivy Bells is uncovered. (p. 16)
1985: Aldrich Ames reveals to the KGB the names of many CIA assets in Russia. (p. 50)
1989: The Berlin Wall comes down.

2001 (September 11): Terrorists attack the World Trade Center and Pentagon with three hijacked planes. A fourth plane crashes in Pennsylvania.

2001: The USA Patriot Act broadens the powers of the police, FBI, and CIA to combat terrorism.

1943: The Colossus is born at **Bletchley Park**. The machine helps the British break German codes. (p. 37)

1943: Major William Martin (**Operation Mincemeat**) floats toward the Spanish shore. (p. 60)

1944 (June 6): Allied troops land in Normandy, France (**D-Day**). (p. 56)

1945: The **Cold War** officially begins.

1947: The National Security Act establishes the National Security Council and the Central Intelligence Agency (CIA).

1949: The Soviet Union becomes a nuclear power.

1950–1953: The Korean War

1952: "**The Thing**" is discovered. (p. 65)

1960: Top-secret CORONA spy satellite launches.

1961: Berlin Wall is built.

1962: The Cuban Missile Crisis (p. 28)

1963: Oleg Penkovsky ("the spy who saved the world") is executed by the KGB. (p. 86)

1991: The Soviet Union and the KGB collapse, signaling the end of the Cold War.

1995 (April 19): A federal building in Oklahoma City is bombed.

2001: FBI special agent **Robert Hanssen**, who is secretly working for Russian intelligence, is arrested after filling a dead drop in Virginia. (p. 53)

2003: The Department of Homeland Security is established.

2004: Post of DNI is created.

2005: The NSA's domestic surveillance program is revealed, allowing the agency to eavesdrop on any communication in America without a legal warrant as long as one party is outside of the United States.

TIGHT PANTS AND
Disguises and Covers

FORGET WHO YOU ARE. You must *live* your "cover." Your life may depend upon convincing people that your disguise is real. It's an upside-down world driven by deception and imagination. What's in your pockets? The coins, keys, ticket stubs, and receipts (called pocket litter) must support your story. If you're suspected, you must continue to *be* your disguise. Don't change a detail! It's your best hope.

The agency has provided you with a false passport, driver's license, and library card. You have a small camera (most spies don't carry weapons) and a few tools: a reversible raincoat, a wig, and makeup. The U.S. government's spy manual says, "Never use a disguise except as a last resort—but when you do, play it for all it's worth."

You're being followed. Now, remove your coat or turn it inside out. Sunglasses? Cap or wig? Put them on or take them off. Slip a pebble into your shoe to change the way you walk or take longer strides. Suddenly, you're someone else.

In 1754, Chevalier d'Eon de Beaumont posed as a woman to get close to the Russian Tsarina Elizabeth. (It wasn't difficult, as his mother often dressed him as a girl.) Renowned lover Giovanni Giacomo Casanova posed as a Venetian sea captain in 1757 and spied for the King of France. Sir Paul Dukes escaped from Russia by pretending to be a member of the secret police, then a man with a bad leg, and finally, an intellectual with a cough.

In some cases, a profession may be a cover. For example, the photographer Alexander Gardner used his camera to gather information for the Union generals. A member of an intelligence agency or the military who steals secrets also uses his profession to gather information. He masquerades as a regular employee, but really acts as a foreign agent or mole.

GIACOMO CASANOVA

Jacques (Giacomo) Casanova visited and was entertained by the captains of the British fleet at Dunkirk. He said, "I found plenty of young officers delighted to show their own importance, who gossiped without needing any encouragement from me." Later, Casanova reported on the strength and discipline of the British fleet to the King of France.

POCKET LITTER

JOSEPH D. STAFFORD

KATHLEEN F. STAFFORD

HENRY LEE SCHATZ

MERCI CANADA

THANKS CANADA

CANADIAN CAPER IN IRAN

In 1979, Iranian revolutionary students attacked the U.S. embassy in Tehran and took fifty-two Americans hostage. Six diplomats escaped and were hidden by Canadian diplomats. CIA chief of disguise Antonio Mendez conducted an operation to rescue them. First, the agency leased studio space in Hollywood. Then they ran photos and announcements of a movie called *Argo* in entertainment newspapers. Finally, a CIA team flew to Iran pretending to be a Hollywood film crew scouting locations for the movie. The consul general was transformed into a flamboyant movie director in tight pants, gold chains, and an "Elvis hairdo." The other conservative diplomats were also disguised as Hollywood types. The "film crew" escaped to Canada with the help of Canadian ambassador Kenneth Taylor. The successful mission was kept secret for seventeen years.

Clockwise: Key casting kit, button compass, lock picks, compass cuff link, disguise kit, and hollow Soviet coins

In the CIA, as in the rest of the country, it became more difficult for women to move into responsible positions after the war. In peacetime, our society somehow felt it could afford the luxury of wasting the talents of women and leaving the Virginia Halls of this world deep in the file drawer.

—*Nora Slatkin*, CIA (Hall spent the last nine years of her career sitting at a desk at the CIA in Washington, D.C.)

A woman who is transformed with makeup and disguises

Know the character or characters you will have to be, inside and out—their clothes, facial expressions, gait, gestures, personal habits, thoughts, and reactions.

—*Manual on Personal Disguise,* U.S. Office of Strategic Services

Classified: a designation that refers to the information in a document or file, and limits readership to individuals with the requisite security clearance (there are three levels of classified information: confidential, secret, and top secret)

Cover: a false identity or occupation assumed by an intelligence officer

Legend: a false life and background

Dead drop: a place where a delivery is made (either documents or payment)

Double agent: an agent of one intelligence service who is secretly working for another

Mole: an agent of an intelligence agency who is working undercover in an enemy's government, military, or intelligence organization

Pocket litter: items in a spy's pocket that support the cover or legend

Spy (asset, informant, source)**:** a person who works covertly for an intelligence agency (usually not a staff member)

Special agent: a staff employee of the FBI

Station: an overseas office of the CIA (typically not identified)

3

JOURNALIST AND PEASANT:

THE NAZIS CREATED A SKETCH OF VIRGINIA HALL. It showed a handsome woman with dark brown hair falling to her shoulders. The Gestapo circulated the picture with instructions: "The woman who limps is one of the most dangerous Allied agents in France. We must find and destroy her."

Virginia Hall was born in 1906 in Baltimore, Maryland. Nicknamed Dindy, she loved baseball and hockey, and going to the shows in her father's movie house. On the family farm, she milked cows, unaware that twenty years later cows would be part of her cover in Nazi-occupied France. Dindy studied languages and became fluent in French, German, and Italian. Her mother insisted that nothing you learn in life is ever wasted.

At twenty-five, Hall became a clerk in the American embassy in Warsaw, Poland. One weekend, she went snipe hunting with friends. Her gun slipped, fired, and sprayed her left foot with shot. By the time she saw a doctor, her foot was gangrenous. As a result, her leg had to be amputated below the knee. Hall received a wooden leg, which she named Cuthbert.

When the war broke out, Hall was in Paris. She joined the Ambulance Service Unit, but fled when France fell to the Germans. In London, she was recruited by the British intelligence service, the SOE, and trained in weaponry, communications, and security. She returned to France posing as a reporter for the *New York Post*.

The American woman organized a resistance network in Vichy, arranged for dead drops for money and weapons, and enlisted citizens to provide safe houses. She also helped escaped prisoners and downed flyers get back to England. When large numbers of Germans marched into Vichy in 1941, Hall was ordered to leave. She climbed over the Pyrenees with three companions in the middle of winter—a grueling trek, especially with a wooden leg! "Cuthbert is giving me trouble, but I can cope," she radioed to London. The operator's response must have amused Hall: "If Cuthbert is giving you trouble, have him eliminated."

VIRGINIA HALL RECEIVING MEDALS
Virginia Hall received the Distinguished Service Cross from "Wild Bill" Donovan in 1945. Donovan wanted President Truman to award the medal, but Hall objected, "refusing any publicity on the grounds that she was 'still operational and most anxious to get busy.'" She also received a Member of the Order of the British Empire from King George VI.

Virginia Hall

Virginia Hall returned to England in November 1943. She requested training as a wireless operator and transferred to the American intelligence service, the OSS. She was given a suitcase filled with full skirts and bulky sweaters to make her young figure appear middle-aged, and her hair was dyed a dirty gray-black. She returned to France by British torpedo boat, because parachuting with a wooden leg was too difficult.

For the next six months, Hall organized, armed, and trained three units of three hundred agents. Her teams blew up bridges, sabotaged rail lines, and disrupted enemy communications. Dressed as a peasant with a staff, she tended goats and noted German troop activities. Driving a donkey cart filled with canisters of goats' milk, she made contact with members of the Resistance. Herding cows to pasture, she picked out locations for parachute drops. Hiding in haylofts, she sent information to London, the French Resistance, and Allied troops. The Gestapo was a step behind her, tracking her radio signals, but they never caught the "limping lady."

 Virginia Hall on a farm

Comint: intelligence gathered from intercepted communications

Elint: electronic intelligence usually collected by technical interception

Humint: intelligence gathered by people

Imint: imagery intelligence gathered by cameras

Photint: photographic intelligence, usually involving high-altitude reconnaissance using spy satellites or aircraft

Radint: intelligence gathered from radar

Sigint: signals intelligence, gathered by intercepting signals

Techint: technical intelligence (equipment and new weapons)

GATHERING INFORMATION

WHY SPY? The first spy scrambled up the tree, leaned out over the wall, and watched his neighbor because he wanted to better his situation. (If he could steal another farmer's secrets, he could have great goats, too!) The first mention of spies in the Bible is in the Book of Genesis: "You are spies. You have come to see the weakness of the land." Was this passage referring to farmers, soldiers, or soldiers disguised as farmers?

In war, intelligence about an enemy's movements, capabilities, or weaknesses helps leaders anticipate what will happen next. The advantage often leads to victory. In peacetime, intelligence can be just as important. It can reveal when an enemy is telling the truth or bluffing, threatening with no plan of attack or quietly preparing to strike. Also, intelligence helps government leaders determine policies toward other nations.

During the Cold War, visitors to the U.S. ambassador's residence in Moscow were handed a small card. They read the four neat sentences in silence:

Every room is monitored by the KGB and all of the staff are employees of the KGB.
We believe the garden also may be monitored. Your luggage may be searched two or
three times a day. Nothing is ever stolen and they hardly disturb things.

At about the same time, Soviet scientists toured a Grumman aircraft plant in Long Island. They put adhesive tape on their shoes to collect slivers of metal alloys being used on new fighter planes. When a runner standing on second base steals signs from a catcher, he is a spy, as is the mole in the technology company who steals designs for a computer chip. The biblical spies, the KGB, the Soviet scientists, the athlete, and the mole are all gathering intelligence. Often they are working for someone else: a spymaster.

One of the earliest known spymasters was Sun Tzu, "Master Sun." The Chinese general wrote eloquently and at length about spying in the fifth century BCE. "Know your enemy," he advised. His book, *The Art of War*, is still read by commanders of military services around the world—and by businesspeople looking to outwit competitors.

Illustration of Sun Tzu on horseback

The Art of War (in Chinese, with its carrying case, and in English)

If one could always be acquainted beforehand with the enemy's designs, one would always beat him with an inferior force.

—*Frederick the Great*

Perhaps the greatest spymaster of the seventeenth century was Cardinal Richelieu. He set up a Cabinet Noir (black chamber) to intercept letters and steal secrets for the French king. He also received reports from an army of spies throughout Europe, including dancing and fencing instructors in the royal courts. Richelieu was despised and often targeted for assassination, but his innovations helped France dominate Europe for more than two centuries.

Who was the first known American spymaster? The answer may be a surprise. It was the man who said, "I cannot tell a lie."

Triple portrait of Richelieu

It is pardonable to be defeated, but never to be surprised.
—*Attributed to Frederick the Great, Napoleon, the U.S. Cavalry, and others*

THE CULPER SPY RING

DURING THE AMERICAN REVOLUTION, the Continental Army led by General George Washington faced a British military that was larger and better trained. Washington knew that he would lose unless he could get information about the numbers, movements, and strategies of his enemy. Spying was considered ungentlemanly—soldiers were supposed to fight on the battlefields, where they could be seen—but the general needed an advantage. So he became a spymaster.

In 1778, the British were headquartered in New York City. Troops arrived by ship from England and marched up the docks. Robert Townsend was also on the waterfront buying items for his dry goods shop. As he picked through the imported merchandise, he observed the ships and listened to the chatter of the soldiers.

Townsend wrote coded messages in Jay's Sympathetic Stain (see box below) and handed them to fellow spy Austin Roe. The second spy unhitched his horse in front of the shop and rode fifty-five miles to a meadow above Conscience Bay, Long Island. Pretending to tend to a herd of cows, Roe placed the letters in a box buried in the ground. The owner of the farm retrieved them. With a telescope, the farmer looked across the bay at a neighbor's clothesline. A black petticoat swinging in the breeze meant that Caleb Brewster had arrived. The number of handkerchiefs on the line indicated the cove where Brewster was waiting. After dark, the farmer delivered the letters to Brewster, who rowed them across Devil's Belt (Long Island Sound). A rider received the dispatch in Fairfield, Connecticut, and relayed it to another rider, who passed it to another, until it arrived at Washington's headquarters. The general sent questions back to Townsend and received replies the same way.

> The CIA has tapped plumbing used by foreign dignitaries . . . Brezhnev and King Farouk . . . and run chemical tests on the contents, searching for the presence of anything suspicious or otherwise informative. The operation requires one agent stationed inside the restroom to signal which facility the dignitary uses.
>
> —*Paul Spinrad*, Research Guide to Bodily Fluids

Jay's Sympathetic Stain: The secret ink that was used to defeat the British was developed by Sir James Jay in London. The ink disappears when it is applied to paper. When a second fluid is brushed across the writing, the words reappear. The formula is still unknown.

The Culper Spy Ring was just one of many spy rings operating in New England and south to the Carolinas. It was America's first intelligence organization. In 1780, Townsend learned that the British were planning a raid on Newport, Rhode Island. The attack would coincide with the arrival of 7,600 French troops to bolster the tattered Continental Army. Washington wrote a letter detailing his plans to invade New York with an army of twelve thousand men. (The general exaggerated considerably.) An agent handed the letter to the British, saying that he had found it on the road. As a result, the British ships changed direction and headed to New York. In Newport, the French ships drifted unopposed into the harbor.

The members of the Culper Spy Ring were never exposed, and remained silent after the Revolution. (Historians learned Townsend's name in 1939, because of a handwriting analysis. The identity of his mistress, who was also an invaluable spy, is still a mystery.) Despite their bravery and successes, the men and women of the Culper Spy Ring would not have been considered heroes during their lifetimes. Spying was just too ungentlemanly. Years later, the British chief of intelligence noted, "Washington did not really outfight the British. He simply outspied us."

THE 33 CONVICTED MEMBERS OF THE DUQUESNE SPY RING

DUQUESNE SPY RING

The Duquesne Spy Ring, named for its leader, Frederick Duquesne, gathered information in New York in the 1930s and '40s. Some of the thirty-three men and women infiltrated shipyards to learn about shipping schedules, sailing routes, and cargoes. They worked in factories and stole secrets about new technologies. The intelligence was communicated via shortwave radio to the Abwehr. Double agent William Sebold was invaluable to the FBI in rounding up and cracking the Duquesne Spy Ring.

LUCY SPY RING

The Lucy Spy Ring gathered information from members of the German High Command, including the exact date and battle plans for the German invasion of Russia in June 1941. Ring member Alexander Foote radioed the secrets to Moscow.

To— Mr. Nathl. Sacket.

Sir,

The advantages of obtaining the earliest and best Intelligence of the designs of the Enemy — the good Character given of you by Colo. Duer added to your capacity for an undertaking of this kind have induced me to entrust the management of this business to your care till further orders on this head.

For your care & trouble in this business I agree on behalf of the public to allow you Fifty Dollars p. Kalender Month — & herewith give you a warrant on the Pay master Genl. for the Sum of Five hund. Dollars to pay those whom you may find necessary to Imploy in the transaction of this business — An acct. of the disbursements of which you are to render to me

Given under my hand at Morris Town this 4th day of Feby. 1777.

G Washington

11

INTERVIEW WITH GENERAL GEORGE WASHINGTON

The general's responses are actual quotations. Of course, the interview is imaginary.

How important is espionage?
There is nothing more necessary than good intelligence to frustrate a designing enemy, and nothing that requires greater pains to obtain.

The great spymaster George Washington

Do you have spies everywhere?
Wherever their army lies, it [is] of greatest advantage to us, to have spies among them. . . . I keep people constantly on Staten Island, who give me daily information of the operations of the enemy.

Do you assume the British are spying on you, too?
There is one evil that I dread, and that is their spies. . . . I think it a matter of some importance to prevent them from obtaining intelligence of our situation.

How would you describe your spies?
Ambiguous characters.

How important is the information that you're receiving?
Even minutiae should have a place in our collection, for things of a seemingly trifling nature when enjoined with others of a more serious cast may lead to valuable conclusions.

Doesn't spying cost a lot of money? What do you tell your generals?
Do not stick at expense to bring this to pass [to find willing spies], as I was never more uneasy than on account of my want of knowledge. [Washington paid $17,000 for intelligence.]

What do you think of General Benedict Arnold, commander of the fort at West Point?

Surely a more active, a more spirited, and more sensible officer fills no department of the army. [Washington was not aware that Arnold was a British spy.]

What do you perceive to be the biggest problem with spying?

From our present position the intelligence is so long getting to hand that it is of no use by the time it reaches me. The good effect of intelligence may be lost if it is not speedily transmitted.

How has your spy network been successful?

We are deceiving our enemies with false opinions of our numbers.

In effect, you are spreading lies. Is this a problem for you? What do you tell your spies about lying?

Keep it within the bounds of what may be thought reasonable or probable.

What about secrets? Do you keep secrets even from your generals?

There are some secrets, on the keeping of which so depends, oftentimes, the salvation of an army: secrets which cannot, at least ought not, to be entrusted to paper; nay, which none but the commander in chief at the time should be acquainted with. . . . For upon secrecy, success depends in most enterprises of the kind, and for want of it, they are generally defeated, however well planned.

Do you have anything more to add?

Everything, in a manner, depends upon obtaining intelligence.

> **Though the commander-in-chief had to approve many death sentences, Arnold was the only man he ever really wanted to hang.**
>
> —*John Bakeless,* Turncoats, Traitors and Heroes

BENEDICT ARNOLD

In 1780, Benedict Arnold, the commander of the fort at West Point, was a British spy. He offered to surrender the West Point territory and forts (and perhaps George Washington) for a large sum of money and equal rank in the British Army. When the plot was discovered, Arnold fled, and was never caught.

LISTEN!

Bugs, Radios, and Transmitters

HOW DO YOU GATHER INFORMATION? First, you use your eyes. In the eighteenth and nineteenth centuries, spies used the "clothesline code." The number of petticoats or handkerchiefs on a clothesline communicated a message. One lantern in the steeple of a church in Boston meant that the British were coming by land. Today, spies and terrorists gather intelligence and correspond on the Internet.

Then, you listen. In the sixteenth century, Catherine de Medici had *auriculaires* (tubes) installed in the palace walls, so that she could eavesdrop on conversations in the next room. (You've heard the expression "the walls have ears"?) In the twentieth century, the CIA used electronic bugs, microphones, and recorders in the same way.

During World War II, citizens were warned about the danger of making casual remarks. It was dangerous to mention to a friend that a loved one was shipping out to war, for if a spy was listening, the ship could be attacked. The War Department produced posters reminding Americans, "Loose lips sink ships."

Listening devices have evolved from ears to *auriculaires* to "bugs" to spy satellites. Today, a bug can be as thin as a human hair. Each new device forces the surprised spy and intelligence agency to invent another device for locating it. At the moment, governments everywhere are listening. Intelligence is being gathered in restaurants, in tunnels, underwater, and in outer space.

Nagra tape recorder and tree stump listening post

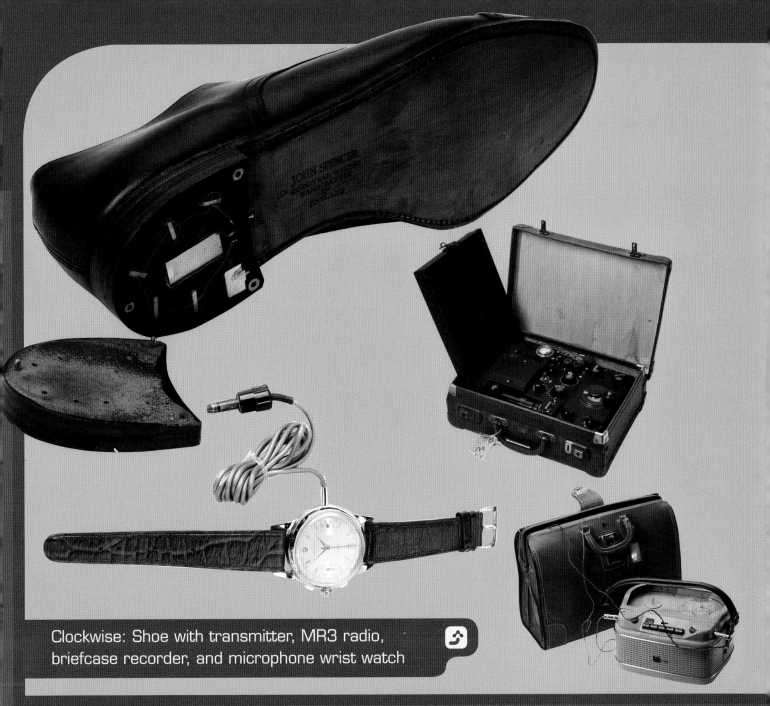

Clockwise: Shoe with transmitter, MR3 radio, briefcase recorder, and microphone wrist watch

They [the CIA] slit the cat open, put batteries in him, wired him up. The tail was used as an antenna. . . . They found he would walk off the job when he got hungry, so they put another wire in to override that. . . . They took it to a park and pointed it at a park bench . . . and a taxi comes and runs him over. There they were sitting in the van with all those dials, and the cat was dead!

—*Victor Marchetti*, CIA official

LISTENING FOUR HUNDRED FEET DOWN
Operation Ivy Bells

IN THE EARLY 1970s, Captain James F. Bradley was sitting in his office at the National Security Agency (NSA). It was three o'clock in the morning, and he was trying to figure out how to find a five-inch cable at the bottom of the Sea of Okhotsk off the coast of the Soviet Union. Bradley was convinced that the Soviets had an underwater communications cable running from their missile submarine base in Petropavlovsk to their headquarters in Vladivostok. Then the captain remembered something from his childhood: the signs on the bank of the Mississippi river that said, "Cable Crossing, Do Not Anchor." Why wouldn't the Soviets need signs, too?

The USS *Halibut* was a lumpy-looking submarine. Under one lump, it had underwater cameras called fish and a large Univac computer. Under another, there was a decompression and lockout chamber allowing Navy divers to enter and exit underwater. It took a month for the sub to get to the Soviet-controlled Sea of Okhotsk, and a week to find the signs. The cameras drifted through the murky water four hundred feet below the surface and discovered a bump in the sand. Navy divers slid out of the chamber and attached a three-foot-long listening device to the cable. After a few hours, they retrieved it.

Most of the conversations on the recordings weren't encoded, because the Russians were convinced no one was listening. When the words were translated, they revealed Soviet intentions, assessments, and fears. The NSA was ecstatic. They commissioned a larger device called a "pod" that could record a month's worth of communications. It was twenty feet long, three feet wide, and weighed six tons. The USS *Halibut* headed west with the pod. The operation was code-named Ivy Bells.

In 1981, the USS *Seawolf*, which had replaced the outdated *Halibut*, fell onto the Soviet cable. Within hours, spy satellites spotted Soviet warships and a salvage ship anchored above the pod. Clearly, the submarine's blunder had led the Soviets to the listening device, but the NSA was confused. The ships arrived too quickly. How could they have mobilized and gotten to the site so soon after the *Seawolf*'s mistake? Four years later, Vitaly Yurchenko, a top KGB officer, defected and provided evidence that a former NSA employee was a Soviet mole. Ronald W. Pelton had exposed Ivy Bells for $35,000.

At the International Spy Museum in Washington, D.C., visitors gaze at a photo of the USS *Halibut* and learn about a top-secret operation called Ivy Bells. At another museum in Moscow, visitors stare at a large, odd-looking device retrieved from the Sea of Okhotsk.

The USS *Halibut*

VITALY YURCHENKO

Vitaly Yurchenko, a twenty-five-year veteran of the KGB, secretly defected to the U.S. in 1985. A few months later, Yurchenko left a Georgetown restaurant, walked to the Soviet Embassy, and claimed he'd been drugged and kidnapped by the CIA. Was Yurchenko a genuine defector? Some speculate that the Soviet staged his defection to help keep Aldrich Ames from being exposed (see page 50). Others believe he just changed his mind. According to the CIA, Yurchenko provided invaluable information while he was in custody.

SMILE...CLICK!
Cameras

"WE HAVE FOUND THE TRACKS of thirty-two men and three donkeys." In 2000 BCE, intelligence reports were gathered by men who counted prints of human feet and donkey hooves. The Lord told Moses to send spies into Canaan to see if the people were "strong or weak, few or many." Before he crossed the Alps on armored elephants (ca. 183 BCE), the spymaster Hannibal received descriptions of the fertility of the plains and the preparations of the Roman soldiers. Imagine if they'd had cameras!

Since the nineteenth century, cameras have recorded and revealed secrets. As technology has become more sophisticated, equipment has gotten smaller. ("Bugs" have also shrunk.) When Alexander Gardner photographed captured agents during the Civil War, he needed a wagon to carry his equipment. In the 1940s, spies took photos with fountain pens, watches, cigarette lighters, and key chains. Cuckoo clocks, umbrellas, glue sticks, and lipsticks also have recorded images. In the 1970s, buttons on an overcoat clicked. Gardner's images were made on large pieces of glass. Today, spies print entire documents on microdots the size of commas or periods. The photos may be hidden in cuff links or tucked behind a stamp on a postcard.

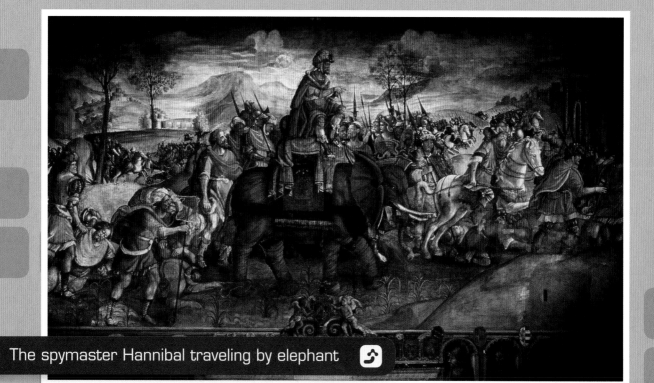

The spymaster Hannibal traveling by elephant

Clockwise from top: Microdot camera, coat-concealed camera, cigarette lighter camera, necktie camera, Steineck wristwatch, fountain pen camera, and key chain camera.

JOHN ANTHONY WALKER, JR., leaned over classified documents from the U.S. Navy. He extended the cord from his Minox camera to the pages. When the lens was the length of the cord away from the pages, the letters and numbers were in focus. Walker spent hours photographing one document after another for the Soviets.

On his last night as a free man, Walker climbed into his van after midnight. He drove to a specific location on a country road. There, he spotted a 7-Up can sitting upright. It was a signal that the KGB was ready. Walker drove to another location and placed a 7-Up can in the gravel, indicating that he was ready. A plastic bag filled with documents covered with trash was left at a third location. At a fourth, Walker expected to find a trash bag with money, but there was none.

Walker was a volunteer Soviet spy from 1967 to 1985. He was the head of a spy ring that eventually included his only son, Michael, his brother, Arthur, and his best friend, Jerry Whitworth. The Walker Spy Ring was devastating, because of the extent of the information in the trash bags. For example:

1. Walker handed over the codes required to launch U.S. nuclear missiles.

2. The KGB received documents describing U.S. troop movements in Vietnam. As the Soviets were allied with the North Vietnamese, they probably shared the information. If so, many American GIs were probably wounded or killed as a result.

Kmart has better security than the Navy.

—John Anthony Walker

WALKER BRIEFCASE/ELECTRONIC COUNTERMEASURES KIT, 1980s
The equipment in Walker's briefcase was used to search for hidden listening devices.

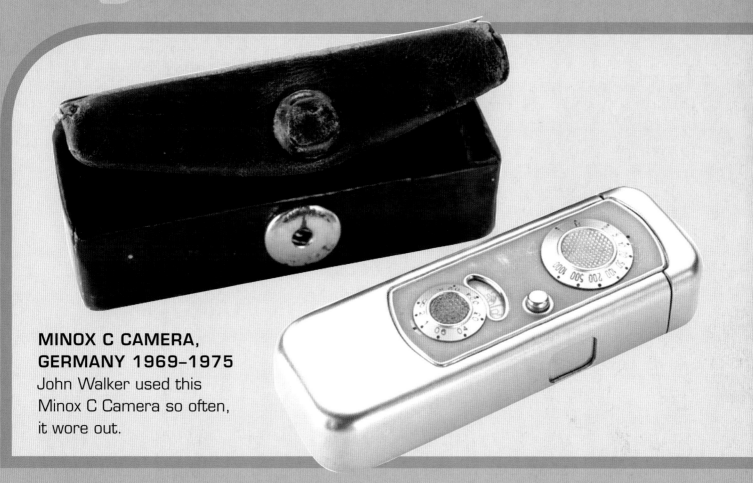

**MINOX C CAMERA,
GERMANY 1969–1975**
John Walker used this
Minox C Camera so often,
it wore out.

3. The KGB learned how U.S. spy satellites could be sabotaged.

4. If a war broke out between the U.S. and the Soviets, the KGB knew how the U.S. would attack and where U.S. submarines would be hiding. The information helped the Soviets strengthen their defenses.

5. A report detailed problems with the nuclear Tomahawk land-attack cruise missile, one of America's most valuable weapons.

6. Another report described the offensive and defensive capabilities of the U.S. Navy's most modern weapon system aboard the USS *Nimitz*.

7. Military data detailed the true capabilities and vulnerabilities of the U.S. Navy.

John Walker in chains after his arrest →

As a Navy radioman, John Walker not only handled classified communications, he was also privy to the codes and keys used to decipher the transmissions. Early in his career, he read the top-secret Single Integrated Operational Plan. If the U.S. was forced to go to war with the Soviets, SIOP outlined the Navy's plan of attack. Walker wondered what the Russians would pay for the information. Motivated solely by greed, the radioman walked into the Soviet Embassy in Washington, D.C., in 1967 and offered his services. Over eighteen years, he provided the KGB with approximately 1 million documents (an average of one hundred and fifty per day). Once the Soviets had the codes, they had access to all encrypted messages, as well as an ability to understand future communications.

A few months before his arrest, John Walker's son, Michael, was awarded "Yeoman of the Quarter" for his outstanding performance in the Navy. Michael was in charge of getting rid of "burn bags" (trash bags filled with classified documents) on board the USS *Nimitz*. Instead, he removed the documents and stored them in his own burn bag until he was ready to leave the ship. Then he carried pounds of materials in a duffel bag to his proud father. Michael was twenty-two when he was arrested. During his interrogation, he pointed out that his Social Security number began with 007.

In 1985, John Walker's wife dialed the FBI and told them her husband was a spy. When the four traitors were arrested, it put an end to "one of the greatest espionage successes in intelligence history," according to *both* sides. Former KGB General Oleg Kalugin marveled at what the radioman had accomplished. "We could have delivered a preemptive strike," he said.

ALEXANDER GARDNER

ALEXANDER GARDNER dabbled in jewelry and finance before deciding on journalism. In 1851, the Scotsman was a reporter and editor at the *Glasgow Sentinel*, but he was dissatisfied. The twenty-nine-year-old was curious about a new invention and a relatively new country. With his mother, brother, wife, and children, he set sail for America. In New York, he got a job assisting the well-known photographer Mathew Brady.

When the Civil War broke out in 1861, Gardner headed for the battlefields with his large camera, glass negatives, ungainly tripod, and horse-drawn darkroom. The Scotsman, who is considered "America's first photojournalist," used his camera to document the war and spy for the Union. In addition to warfare and corpses, Gardner photographed maps, documents, battle sites, and troops. Union commanders poured over his images of Confederates, looking for spies and double agents.

After the war, Gardner invented a way to identify criminals for the Washington Police Department: the mug shot. He also photographed the American West. Twenty years after his death, a scrap dealer bought ninety thousand glass negatives. The images taken by Gardner and many early photographers included the Battle of Gettysburg, President Lincoln, and other images of nineteenth-century America. When the dealer couldn't find a buyer, he scrubbed off the faces and battle scenes, and sold the glass.

ALEXANDER GARDNER

This image of Alexander Gardner was taken in Washington, D.C., in 1863, about the time his gallery opened on Seventh Avenue and D Street. Gardner took many photos of Abraham Lincoln, and allegedly photographed the president the day he was assassinated in 1865.

GARDNER'S PHOTO OF JOHN WILKES BOOTH

Alexander Gardner photographed the well-known actor John Wilkes Booth. One image was later used on his "Wanted" poster.

SPIES IN THE SKIES

"MAN MUST RISE ABOVE THE EARTH," Socrates said around 400 BCE, ". . . for only then will he fully understand the world in which he lives." Understanding was not the only reason to get off the ground. An aerial view provided a way of spying on the enemy. According to Chinese and Japanese folklore, "spotters" rose into the air attached to kites.

During the Civil War, seamstresses made balloons (sometimes from recycled silk dresses) for the Union and the Confederacy. Three hundred feet above the ground, soldiers sketched maps and reported enemy activity. The intelligence was transmitted to ground troops over telegraph lines. Balloons were also used for spying in the Franco-Prussian War, the American Civil War, and World War I. In 1947, large balloons fitted with cameras drifted over the Soviet Union. The operation was code-named Moby Dick. Of course, fog, wind, and bullets were always a problem.

Pigeons have carried messages for centuries. During World War I, they also took photographs. The French government declared that anyone who stopped the dependable "racehorses of the sky" in flight could be sentenced to death, but everyone shot at them. The birds had great names like "The Mocker" (who flew fifty-two missions), "President Wilson," and "GI Joe."

Throughout the Cold War, the U.S. government was concerned about a Soviet attack. Spy planes invaded Soviet airspace and took photos of shipyards, fighter jets, and missile sites. In one month in 1952, the planes flew 1,750 missions and produced 65,000 photographs! Sometimes the planes would pop up visibly in Soviet airspace, provoking Moscow, but they were slow and unarmed. Between 1950 and 1970, 252 American airmen were shot down. At least one pilot ate his top-secret papers as he parachuted to earth. Today, 138 men are still missing.

The Soviets couldn't retaliate, because they didn't have air bases close enough to the United States. Instead, they developed spy satellites. In October 1957, *Sputnik I* flew into space. It was the size of a basketball, weighed 183 pounds, and orbited the earth in ninety-eight minutes. Four months later, the United States launched *Explorer I*. Suddenly, the superpowers were engaged in a new war—in space. By January 2003, there were 2,816 active satellites and 6,200 obsolete satellites, rockets, and launchers twirling high above the clouds. How many spy satellites are watching you? No one knows.

CHRISTOPHER BOYCE

Christopher Boyce, the son of an FBI agent, worked for an aerospace company that helped run U.S. spy satellites. Upset with U.S. policy overseas, particularly the Vietnam War, Boyce and a boyhood buddy passed films to the KGB. Both were convicted and imprisoned in 1977.

British observer leaping from his balloon (WWI)

Balloon Co. balloon being brought down

We saw that the aeroplane would give eyes to armies, and the armies with the most eyes would win the war [World War I].

—*Orville Wright*

Pigeon being released from tank in northern France during WWI

Three pigeons wearing cameras

CHER AMI (–1919)

On October 4, 1918, an American battalion was surrounded by Germans in the Argonne Forest. The soldiers' last hope was a Black Check Cock carrier pigeon named Cher Ami. With a canister attached to his left leg, the pigeon rose into the air. The German infantry saw the bird and fired. Cher Ami was hit in the breast and leg, but managed to recover and fly twenty-five miles in twenty-five minutes. He lost his leg (several soldiers made him a wooden leg later) and was blinded in one eye, but he saved 194 lives. On June 13, 1919, the little hero died of his war wounds. He was stuffed and given to the National Museum of American History in Washington, D.C.

TAXIDERMIED PIGEON WITH CAMERA
Hundreds of thousands of pigeons were used for military communication and photography. Despite enemy fire, 95 percent of the carrier pigeons completed their missions.

THE CUBAN MISSILE CRISIS

IN AUGUST 1962, U-2 spy planes cruised over Cuba and took photographs. Analysts inspected the images and discovered new construction on surface-to-air missile (SAM) bases. They compared the aerial photos to manuals of Soviet SAM sites provided by GRU colonel Oleg Penkovsky who was spying for the CIA (see page 86), and found they were identical. Could the Soviets be planning to install missiles with nuclear warheads in Cuba, ninety miles from the United States?

The number of spy plane missions over Cuba doubled. New aerial images showed more SAM sites as well as Soviet high-performance fighter airplanes. At the time, there were more than two thousand ships in the Atlantic Ocean that could have been carrying the nuclear warheads to the island. On October 22, President Kennedy announced that the U.S. Navy would stop and search all ships headed to Cuba. (Secretly, he sent U-2 photos to Britain, Canada, France, and West Germany to get international support for his actions.) Kennedy added that the launch of any missile would be considered a Soviet attack and lead to a strike on Moscow.

At first, the Soviets were silent. The U.S. military went on high alert. Thousands of Americans sat motionless in front of black-and-white television sets and prayed. Soviet and U.S. nuclear submarines shadowed each other in the deep water. Five days after Kennedy's announcement, an American U-2 was shot down over Cuba by a Soviet missile. Many people believed World War III was inevitable.

On the morning of October 28, the Soviets agreed to disassemble the missile sites and remove the rockets. Two U.S. spy planes brought back photographs confirming that the sites were being taken apart. Later, U.S. Navy planes spotted Soviet freighters headed east with large missiles on their decks.

RQ-1 PREDATOR
When there is concern of contamination by biological or chemical weapons, the U.S. Defense Department uses an unmanned aircraft such as the RQ-1 Predator. The plane was developed in the mid-1990s for medium-altitude intelligence gathering.

AERIAL RECONNAISSANCE PHOTO OF CUBA

This photo was taken by a U-2 spy plane. It shows Soviet nuclear missiles in Cuba aimed at the United States.

Labels on photo: MISSILE ERECTOR, CABLE, MISSILE SHELTER TENT, TRACKED PRIME MOVERS, OXIDIZER TANK TRAILERS, TANK TRAILERS

Baseball fields perhaps?

—KGB officer Georgi Bolshakov's response when he was shown photos of Cuban missile sites

FRANCIS GARY POWERS

Francis Gary Powers was flying a U-2 spy plane over the Soviet Union when he was shot down on May 1, 1960. The incident led Washington to admit that they were spying and increased tensions with the Soviets. When his son asked, "How high were you flying, Dad?" Powers replied, "Not high enough."

WHAT?

Codes, Code Makers, and Code

BEFORE HUMAN BEINGS COULD READ OR WRITE, they drew pictures. The images of animals, hunters, and spears were symbols. In Egypt, they were called hieroglyphs. Several symbols together could be a decoration—or a coded message. When one language replaced another, the meanings of the symbols often disappeared. For centuries, European explorers were baffled by the repetitive marks on Egyptian tombs.

In 1799, Napoleon's soldiers were enlarging a fort in Rosetta, Egypt. As they moved stones from an old building into place, they discovered a large black rock. It had on it three identical texts in different languages and was dated 196 BCE. A French archaeologist, Jean-Francois Champollion, was the first to use the Rosetta Stone to solve the mystery of the Egyptian hieroglyphs. He discovered that the symbols represented sounds as well as words.

When people learned to read and write, it became more difficult to send private messages. The need for secrecy produced code makers, and the desire to steal those secrets produced code breakers. The study of secret writing, called cryptography, began in the Italian Renaissance. Leon Battista Alberti wrote the first essay on code craft and invented a cipher disk. (It replaces one letter with another. The sender uses it to disguise a message, and the receiver uses the same disk to read the message. Each movement of the disk creates a new code.) Alberti's cipher was used to create codes for more than four hundred years. Thomas Jefferson also invented a cipher disk in the 1790s, very similar to one used by the U.S. Army up until World War II.

There is less danger in fearing too much than too little.

—Sir Francis Walsingham

JULIUS CAESAR
Julius Caesar (100 BCE–44 BCE) used a displacement cipher replacing each letter with the letter that follows it in the alphabet by three places. (A becomes D.) Today, any displacement code may be called a Caesar cipher.

Detail of the Rosetta Stone on display at the British Museum

Words written in code were not the only way to communicate secret information. In 1890, Robert Baden-Powell needed details of an enemy's fortress in the Balkans. Disguised as an entomologist, he sketched butterflies. He drew veins on the butterfly's wings to indicate the plan of the fortifications, and spots to denote the positions and sizes of the guns. The lines on the leaves represented trenches. (Only a real entomologist would have suspected!)

Fifty years later, the Nazis sent letters to French citizens inviting them to meetings of the French Resistance. It was a trick to find out who was part of the underground. If the citizen showed up, he was arrested. If he didn't report the letter to the German authorities, he was suspected of supporting the Resistance. If he did, and the meeting was real, members of the French underground were arrested. British intelligence came up with a solution: a code. They designed a fake postage stamp identical to the real one except that there was a small mark under the lady's left eye. If an invitation arrived without that stamp, it was a Nazi trap.

Postage stamps, invisible inks, and butterflies have changed history. Thousands of lives have been saved by code makers, code breakers, and code talkers. An unpopular queen retained the throne and a beautiful queen lost her head, because the code maker was not quite as clever as the code breaker. Would you bet your life on a code?

This cipher disk was invented by Thomas Jefferson in 1790.

ALEXANDER THE GREAT

Alexander the Great (356–323 BCE) spied on his enemies and his own soldiers. His spies communicated with sky-tales. First, a scroll was wrapped around a stick, then a message was written on it. The scroll was unwrapped and sent off with the spy. If it was intercepted, it couldn't be read without a stick with the same diameter sky-tale.

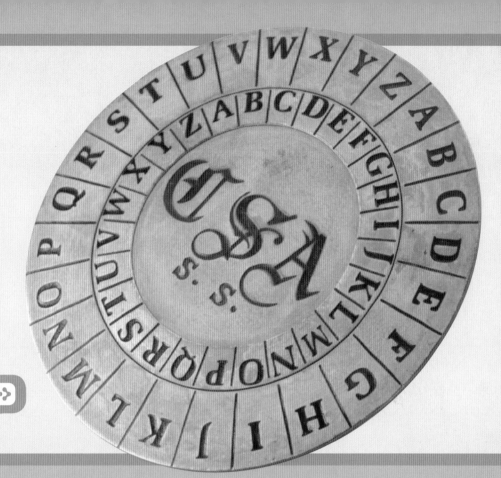

CIPHER DISK

This cipher disk was used to create displacement ciphers. When the inner wheel is turned, the letters of the alphabet align with new ones. Each turn creates a new cipher.

Confederate Civil War cipher disk, 1862

[During World War II, the U.S.] Office of Censorship banned . . . the sending of . . . international chess games . . . crossword puzzles . . . listings of students' grades. One letter containing knitting instructions was held up long enough for an examiner to knit a sweater. . . . Even lovers' Xs, meant as kisses, were heartlessly deleted if censors thought they might be a code.

—*David Kahn,* The Codebreakers

GIOVANNI BATTISTA PORTA

Giovanni Battista Porta, considered the outstanding cryptographer of the Renaissance, invented recipes for invisible inks including one for use on a hard-boiled egg. With invisible ink, Porta wrote a message on the shell of a hard-boiled egg. The message disappeared, but could be read on the white of the egg if it was peeled.

THE BABINGTON PLOT: Mary, Queen of Scots

ON OCTOBER 15, 1586, Mary, Queen of Scots, approached the defendant's seat in Fotheringhay Castle. She was dressed in black velvet and accompanied by her physician. The Scottish queen was on trial for plotting to kill her cousin, Elizabeth I, the Queen of England. Mary knew her life depended on a cipher. If it had been broken, she would be accused of treason and beheaded.

Mary became Queen of Scotland when she was nine months old. She had an arranged marriage at sixteen to the eldest son of the King of France, but her husband died a year later. Her second marriage in 1565 was to a cousin, the Earl of Darnley. They had a son, James VI, but in 1567, Darnley was murdered. The following summer, Protestant nobles imprisoned the Catholic queen and forced her to abdicate the throne to her fourteen-month-old son. Mary tried to regain power, but her army was defeated and she fled.

Mary assumed that her cousin, the Queen of England, would protect her, but she was wrong. Elizabeth I had her own problems. She was the child of the former king's second marriage. Catholics in England didn't recognize her father's divorce from his first wife, so they believed that a child of a second marriage was illegitimate, and therefore, an illegitimate queen. She was also a Protestant. Mary, however, was a Catholic and she had a distant claim to the English throne. So Elizabeth I imprisoned her beautiful cousin.

In sixteenth-century England, Catholics were persecuted. Priests were accused of treason and their protectors tortured. One night, a group of young Catholics plotted to free Mary. Anthony Babington and six conspirators also discussed assassinating Elizabeth I and, with support from abroad, overthrowing the government. A message was written in a cipher alphabet with code words and hidden in the stopper of a beer barrel. It was entrusted to Gilbert Gifford, Mary's courier.

Gifford was a secret agent working for Sir Francis Walsingham, Elizabeth's spymaster. Walsingham also employed Thomas Phelippes, perhaps the finest cryptanalyst in Europe. Of course, Phelippes deciphered the message. Babington's plot didn't implicate Mary, so Walsingham waited for her reply. On July 17, 1586, Mary sent a coded message via Gifford which left the assassination up to the conspirators. Babington and his friends were captured, tortured, and killed, and Mary went on trial.

The judges found Mary guilty of treason. (Was she really guilty, or was she set up by Walsingham? The spymaster had urged Elizabeth I to get rid of her cousin for many years.) Three hundred people gathered for the beheading. Before the axe fell, Mary insisted that she had never authorized the assassination, and prayed aloud for the Catholic Church, her son, and Elizabeth I. A small dog hiding in Mary's petticoats yelped and refused to leave her side.

NON SINE SOLE
IRIS.

QUEEN ELIZABETH I

In this portrait, Queen Elizabeth I wears a gown embroidered with eyes and ears, symbols of espionage. The "Virgin Queen" never produced an heir.

GIROLAMO CARDANO (1501–1576)

Girolamo Cardano was an Italian physician, mathematician, philosopher, astrologer, interpreter of dreams, and cryptographer. He invented the Cardano Grille and an early form of Braille. After reading a book by Cardano, Sir Francis Walsingham became fascinated with codes.

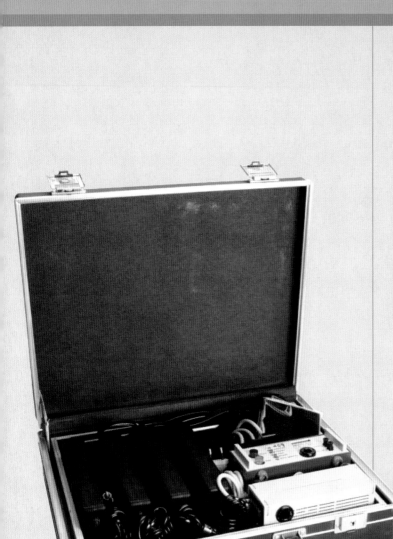

FLAPS AND SEALS KIT, U.S., 1960–1970

Letter tamperers often made a cast of a wax seal, melted the original seal, read the letter, and then made a new seal from the cast.

SECRET WRITING DETECTION KIT, STASI, 1980s

East German intelligence officers used this secret writing detection kit to read secret messages. Their informants were given pens containing special ink that would only fluoresce when viewed under ultraviolet light of a specific wavelength—otherwise, the writing remained invisible.

> Gentlemen do not read each other's mail.
>
> —*U.S. Secretary of State Henry Stimson's explanation for*
> *shutting down the U.S. code-breaking operation in 1929*

BLETCHLEY PARK

WHAT IS AN ENIGMA? It's a puzzle, riddle, or mystery. It was also the name of a Nazi code machine. In the 1940s, before the age of the computer, the Enigma was capable of 150,000,000,000,000,000,000 different combinations. The Germans had good reason to believe that their code would always be a mystery to outsiders.

The Enigma looked like a typewriter, but the keyboard was connected electrically to a series of rotors. Each time a letter was typed, the rotors changed the substitution pattern. The result was sent in Morse code. The receiver's Enigma translated the Morse code back to meaningless words. Because the rotors on the receiver's machine were adjusted the same way as those on the sender's, the words were transposed into the original message. The starting position and connections on the rotors were reset daily.

Eccentric Alan Turing wore a gas mask to prevent hay fever and chained his coffee cup to a radiator, but he was a mathematical genius. At Bletchley Park, a Victorian estate fifty miles north of London, Turing worked to crack the Enigma code with an army of ten thousand code breakers. They included academics, chess players, crossword-puzzle experts, linguists, and artists. Because of the war, many of those working day and night were women.

The original calculating machine used to decipher the Enigma was called the "bombe" (after a contemporary ice cream dessert!). In 1943, design began on the "Colossus," a seven-foot-tall machine that could decipher thousands of codes per minute, including the most complex ones used by the Nazi high command and Hitler. The Colossus was an important step toward the first programmable electronic computer!

Prime Minister Winston Churchill received so much intelligence from the deciphered communications, he called them his "golden eggs." The code breakers were his "geese who laid the golden eggs and never cackled." After the war, ten thousand men and women were sworn to secrecy, the code-breaking machines were dismantled, and the papers were burned. The story of Bletchley Park didn't leak out until thirty years later. Finally, a few geese cackled.

What one man can invent another can discover.

—Sir Arthur Conan Doyle

RED ORCHESTRA

At the beginning of World War II, a Russian spy ring called the Red Orchestra used a code based on books. Telegraph operators (called "pianists") used shortwave radios ("pianos") to broadcast information ("music") about Nazi war plans back to Moscow.

Morse code class

BENJAMIN FRANKLIN

Benjamin Franklin was a key member of the first official organization in America for collecting foreign intelligence, the Committee of Secret Correspondence (established by the Continental Congress in 1775). In 1778, Franklin became ambassador to France. During the Revolutionary War, he pressured the French to create an alliance with the Americans against the British. He also monitored British political and military activities through spies in London.

ENIGMA MACHINE

The Nazis never suspected that the Enigma code had been broken, so they used it throughout the war.

German soldiers sending a secret message with an Enigma machine ➡

CODE BREAKING AT BLETCHLEY PARK

Many historians believe that the Colossus and the code breakers at Bletchley Park probably shortened the war by two years.

FANYS SPECIAL OPERATIONS

In World War I, the British Navy established the Women's Royal Naval Service (WREN) and the First Aid Nursing Yeomanry (FANY) to fill important jobs while men were fighting overseas. In World War II, thousands of the FANYs (below) and WRENs worked at Bletchley Park.

WRENs with torpedo

REMEMBER THE ENEMY IS LISTENING

During World War II, the U.S. Signal Intelligence Service was located in Arlington Hall, a former girls' school in Virginia. William Friedman and his team cracked the Japanese Purple code here on September 20, 1940. The interceptions were called "magic," and the code breakers "magicians." In 1943, Britain and the U.S. signed the first cooperative code-breaking agreement.

NAVAJO CODE TALKERS

THE NAVAJOS HAVE A COMPLEX LANGUAGE. Not only is there no alphabet, but one word can have several unrelated meanings. When the tone (low, high, falling, or rising) changes, so does the meaning. For example, "mouth" becomes "medicine." In the 1940s, the language hadn't been written down or studied, and fewer than twenty-eight Americans (not including the Navajos) could speak it. One was Philip Johnston, a son of missionaries who had grown up on a reservation.

Johnston picked up a newspaper in 1942 and read that the Canadian Army had used Native Americans as "signalmen" during World War I. As a veteran, he knew the importance of secure radio and telephone transmissions. Johnston suggested to a Navy commander that Navajos should be employed as radiomen. They could transmit messages in their remarkable language.

On May 5, 1942, the first twenty-nine Navajos began basic training in San Diego, California. (Between 375 and 420 men would be trained as "code talkers.") When the Navy code talkers needed a word for "dive bomber" they chose *da-he-tih-hi*, the Navajo word for "hummingbird." *Chay-da-gahi*, meaning "tortoise," was code for "tank." (Both have hard shells and often move slowly.) America was *Ne-he-mah*, the Navajo word for "our mother." The Japanese wiretappers were mystified. An expert code breaker said, "It sounded like gibberish. We couldn't even transcribe it, much less crack it."

The code talkers made an invaluable contribution on the front lines in the South Pacific. In the first forty-eight hours of the Battle of Iwo Jima, six Navajos sent more than eight hundred secure messages without a single mistake. When the war ended, the men were sworn to secrecy. They returned to their reservations without any recognition for their service.

Finally, the program was declassified. In 1968, Americans learned how the code talkers were responsible for saving thousands of marines. Thirty-three years later (2001), four of the original twenty-nine Navajos who were still living gathered in the rotunda of the U.S. Capitol. Below paintings of European settlers who had driven the tribes from their homelands, the code talkers received awards from the President of the United States.

NAVAJO CODE TALKERS
Code talkers made an invaluable contribution to the war effort and victory in the Pacific during World War II.

CODED CONVERSATION

IMAGINE TWO BIRD-WATCHERS (SPIES) sitting in a café in Rome in the early 1960s. There is a tall, dark spy (code name: Woodchuck) and a short, blond spy (code name: Marshmallow). The CIA agents are concerned that the café is bugged, so they speak in code.

Woodchuck: What happened in Moscow?

Marshmallow: Ears only.

Woodchuck: Of course.

Marshmallow: I was burned.

Woodchuck: You didn't dry clean?

Marshmallow: Several times.

Woodchuck: Babysitters?

Marshmallow: Nope.

Woodchuck: You had a shoe?

Marshmallow: And an L-pill in my pen. I tried to bite off the end, but they grabbed it.

Woodchuck: Then what happened?

Marshmallow: They duct-taped my hands and mouth and took me to the Center.

Woodchuck: Oh, no. . . .

Marshmallow: First, they wanted to know if I was working for the Skiers. They accused me of being a pianist and started shouting, "Where's your piano?"

Woodchuck: They must have some comint.

Marshmallow: Could be humint or radint, too.

Waiter, check please.

Alpinists: the Americans

Babysitter: bodyguard

Bang and burn: demolition and sabotage operations

Bird-watcher: spy (British slang)

Black bag job: secret entry into a home or office to steal or copy materials

Bride: early code name for the worldwide effort to decipher Soviet transmissions, also the designation for both the collection of these coded messages and the intelligence produced by that effort

Boxers: the French

Burned: when a case officer or agent is compromised

Camp Swampy: the CIA's secret domestic training base

Center: KGB (Soviet Intelligence) headquarters in Moscow

Chicken feed: convincing but not critical intelligence knowingly provided by an agent to an enemy intelligence agency

Cobbler: a spy who fabricates false documents

Comint: all intelligence gathered by intercepted communications

Company (the): CIA's term for itself

One of them said, "Tell me about the bang and burns." Another was screaming about black bag jobs for the Boxers. When I told them they had the wrong guy, I heard the biggest one whisper, "He's a cobbler. Probably works for the Alpinists."

Woodchuck: Didn't you have any lifesavers?

Marshmallow: No. They started asking me about Suntan. Can you believe it?

Woodchuck: We gotta have a mole.

Marshmallow: I started talking. It was just chicken feed, but I told them I could get more information from a floater in Rome.

Woodchuck: They bought it?

Marshmallow: Yup. They even took me to the train station.

Woodchuck: Unbelievable. Did they talk about executive action?

Marshmallow: Over and over, and the hospital . . .

Woodchuck: Are you going back?

Marshmallow: Never. The Company wants me to come home. They say I can work at Camp Swampy, but I'd rather be a handler. Bride interests me, too. But I have to tell you, I learned a real lesson in Moscow.

Woodchuck: What?

Marshmallow: Don't ever go naked.

[The tall, dark bird-watcher nods. His short, blond friend raises his index finger.]

Marshmallow: *Cameriere, il conto per favore.*

Dry clean: actions agents take to determine if one is under surveillance in order to elude it

Ears only: material too secret to commit to writing

Executive action: assassination

Floater: person used for an intelligence operation (maybe a one-time or occasional use)

Handler (or controller): officer in charge of a string of agents

Hospital: prison (Russian slang)

Humint: intelligence collected by human sources

Lifesavers: confidential evidence or documents (often used to ingratiate yourself with a foreign intelligence agency)

L-pill: poison pill used to commit suicide

Mole: a member of one intelligence agency who is secretly working for another

Naked: spy operating without cover or backup

Pianist (or musician): clandestine radio operator

Piano (or music box): clandestine radio

Radint: intelligence gathered from radar

Shoe: false passport or visa operation

Skiers: the British

Suntan: code name for the Lockheed CL-400 spy plane that was proposed as a successor to the U-2 but was never built

ONION SKINS, PUMPKIN PATCHES, AND OTHER HIDING PLACES

THE IMAGINATION IS CRUCIAL to all aspects of espionage, including "hiding places." In the ancient world, spies wrote coded messages on the insides of leather belts. The courtiers of Mary, Queen of Scots, removed messages from the stopper of a beer barrel. Confederate spy Betty Duvall carried dispatches coiled in her hair. During World War II, members of the French Resistance put intelligence inside the handlebars of their bicycles and pedaled past the Gestapo.

Shoes, cuff links, and sheet music have all carried secret messages. A doll tucked under a little girl's arm or an artificial eye may have information inside. During the Cold War, agents hid intelligence inside toilet paper holders on trains passing through East Germany. CIA spy Oleg Penkovsky put film in a box of candies and offered it to children playing in a Moscow park. Of course, they brought it straight to their mother, the wife of a staff member at the British Embassy. Hollow coins are a favorite hiding place, but not for one KGB officer. Late one night, Rudolf Abel's deputy mistakenly paid for a newspaper with a hollow nickel. The coin slipped out of his hand, bounced on the New York pavement, and split open. A microfilm rolled out. Abel was eventually arrested.

WHITTAKER CHAMBERS

Whittaker Chambers, a senior editor at *Time* magazine, confessed to having been a courier for the Soviets in 1939. Nine years later, he revealed that Alger Hiss, a State Department official, was a Soviet spy. Hiss claimed he had never met Chambers. The editor produced the "pumpkin papers," classified documents he had received from Hiss. Chambers had hidden the evidence (actually films of the documents, not papers) in a hollowed-out pumpkin on his family farm. Hiss was convicted of perjury and imprisoned.

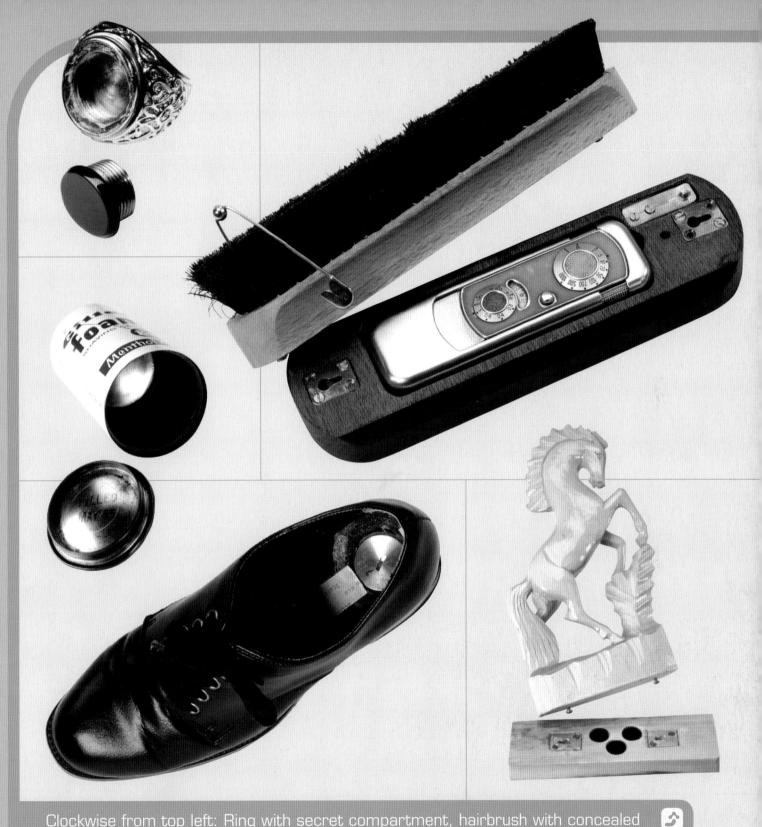

Clockwise from top left: Ring with secret compartment, hairbrush with concealed camera, statuette concealment for Minox camera, courier shoe with container (KGB, 1980s), hollow shaving cream can concealment (U.S., 1960s).

ELIZABETH VAN LEW

AS A YOUNG GIRL, Elizabeth Van Lew heard an unforgettable story. A slave and her baby were sold to different owners. When the mother learned their fate, she dropped dead of a broken heart. "Slave power is cruel," Van Lew told her neighbors in Virginia. People thought the tiny, passionate Southern belle with her blue eyes and bobbing curls was foolish.

The Van Lews lived in a three-story mansion with robust columns, chandeliers, and silk-covered walls. It stood on the highest hill in Richmond, the capital of the Confederacy. The family owned slaves, but Miss Lizzy freed them after her father's death. Then she hired them back. She also bought and freed their relatives, and even paid for one, Mary Bowser, to go to the Quaker Negro School in Philadelphia.

From her garden, Van Lew could see the warehouses where Union soldiers were imprisoned. The fearless woman asked the Confederate commander if she could be a hospital nurse. He was incredulous—why would any Southerner want to help a Yankee?—but he relented.

Miss Lizzy spent her inheritance on books, food, clothes, bedding, and medicines for the wounded and starving prisoners. (She nursed Colonel Paul Revere, the great-grandson of the Revolutionary hero. The young soldier died later at the Battle of Gettysburg.) Van Lew hid coded notes in the spines of books and inside the false bottom of a family platter. Prisoners eavesdropped on the guards and sent information back, written in pinpricks on the pages of the books. Miss Lizzy copied the reports onto onionskins, then slipped them into the boots of her servants. She also tucked messages inside empty eggshells. The ex-slaves moved north along the James River carrying the valuable intelligence to the Union Army. (Ulysses S. Grant often received it along with fresh flowers from Miss Lizzy's garden.)

The clever spy realized that she could avoid suspicion by acting mentally unbalanced. Wearing a battered sunbonnet and her oldest clothes, Van Lew wandered down the sidewalk mumbling conversations

ELIZABETH VAN LEW ONIONSKIN
Elizabeth Van Lew sent a warning to a collaborator on an onionskin.

and singing silly songs. Neighbors called her "Crazy Bet." Everyone knew she was a Union sympathizer, but they didn't take her seriously.

In 1863, Van Lew persuaded Mary Bowser to seek employment in the home of Jefferson Davis, president of the Confederacy. Of course, the Davises assumed that the ex-slave was illiterate. In the library, Bowser scanned documents on Davis's desk. In the dining room, she memorized conversations. When the baker arrived with fresh bread, Bowser met his wagon and told him what she had learned.

Confederates confiscated family horses to replace those killed in battle. Van Lew needed her last horse for her espionage activities. Twice she learned that soldiers were on their way up Church Hill. The first time, she hid the animal in the smokehouse. The second, she led him up the front staircase to the library. The horse stood motionless on a blanket of straw above the soldiers one floor below.

Van Lew often used a cipher for her communications. The key was concealed in her watchcase. Terrified of being discovered, she hid papers in the andirons in her bedroom fireplace and buried her journal in the garden. When the war was over, she petitioned the War Department to turn over the records of her activities so that she could destroy them. She didn't want any of her neighbors to know what she had done.

The Union spy died in poverty in 1900. She was buried vertically (facing north), because there was no room in the Richmond cemetery. When the family of Colonel Paul Revere and Union soldiers in Boston heard that Miss Lizzy didn't leave enough money for a headstone, they bought her one and wrote the inscription themselves.

DEAD DROPS AND SIGNAL SITES

WHAT IS THE GREATEST CHALLENGE IN ESPIONAGE? (Staying alive, perhaps? In a few pages, you will read about brass knuckles, suicide pills, and retribution, but that's not the correct answer.) The greatest challenge is *communication*. What good is a clever spy who discovers an enemy is about to attack, but can't communicate the information? (During the Cold War, it was difficult to get information into or out of the Soviet Union and Soviet-controlled communist countries. Winston Churchill said, "An iron curtain has descended across the continent.")

Spies must communicate quickly. Intelligence agencies often use information to avoid surprise. Intelligence delayed may be useless. Messages implying the Japanese were about to attack Pearl Harbor were deciphered the day before the bombs fell. Regretfully, the information wasn't analyzed and delivered to the proper people in time. In the eighteenth century, General Washington had to be very patient. It took one week for the Culper Spy Ring to get reports from Manhattan to the general's headquarters, and another week to get questions back.

Usually, the spy delivers secrets to a "handler" (a member of the intelligence agency) who turns them over to the agency itself. To maintain secrecy, many spies and their handlers don't meet. Instead, spies may have a "signal site" where they alert their handler that they are ready to make a delivery, and a separate "dead drop" where the delivery is made.

Aldrich Ames made chalk marks on a mailbox to alert his KGB handler. One of John Walker's signals was a 7-Up can at a designated spot on a country road. Robert Hanssen posted multicolored thumbtacks on a sign on Foxhall Road in Washington. All three spies stuffed stolen documents in trash bags and "dropped" them, or hid them in public places. Signal sites and dead drops can be anywhere, inside or out. In the 1770s, Abraham Woodhull of the Culper Spy Ring dug up a box buried in a cow pasture. One hundred and ninety years later, Oleg Penkovsky stuffed film behind a green radiator in a Moscow entryway.

Dead drop spike, CIA, 1960s–1990s

Clockwise from left: Hollow nail concealments (KGB, 1950s), hollow bolt concealment (KGB, 1950s), and hollow rock concealment (CIA, 1960s)

DOG DOO-DOO CONCEALMENT DEVICE, CIA, CIRCA 1970

In order for a concealment device to work, it must be hidden or disguised as something else. A crumpled soda can was once a popular choice, until recycling. What object is the least likely to attract attention in a public park or to be picked up? Dog doo-doo.

ALDRICH AMES

ALDRICH AMES'S FATHER was a CIA operative in Burma in the 1950s. When he told his sixteen-year-old son about his secret life, he said, "You and I both know that lying is wrong, son. . . . It is okay to mislead people if you are doing it in the service of your country, but it is never okay to lie or mislead people for your own personal benefit." Rick Ames wanted to be a CIA officer just like his dad.

In high school, the witty Rick Ames wore a trench coat, went on secret missions, used a coded language, and pretended to be different characters. "Rick got his kicks from fooling people," said a classmate. He worked in a CIA summer job program for children of employees, making fake money for the agency's training facility. When he got to the University of Chicago in 1959, Ames was more interested in the Blackfriars, a student drama group, than his courses. After two years, he flunked out. With his father's help, he got a job as a clerk-typist at the CIA.

In 1967, Ames graduated from George Washington University and entered the CIA's Junior Officer Training program (JOT). Two years later, he was sent to Turkey for his first overseas assignment—recruiting Soviet and East European informants. Ames was so unsuccessful, he considered quitting. When he returned home, he discovered that his application to foreign language school had been accepted. Soon he was studying Russian.

In New York City, Ames was assigned to handle the case of Sergei Fedorenko. The Russian was a nuclear arms expert and a member of the Soviet delegation to the United Nations. Fedorenko had been pressured to spy for the KGB, but he hated the Soviet intelligence agency, so he volunteered to work secretly for the CIA and FBI. The handler and the Soviet spy became close friends who trusted each other completely. "I will work with you. I am placing my life in your hands. Please don't screw up," Sergei told Rick.

In the early eighties, Ames's marriage fell apart and his career stalled. He drank heavily and complained about U.S. foreign policy to his colleagues. His life changed when he met a cultural specialist at the Colombian Embassy in Mexico City. Maria del Rosario Casas Dupuy was a member of a prominent family, and a low-level CIA informant. The two fell madly in love.

In 1983, Ames was promoted to counterintelligence branch chief in Soviet operations. The position at CIA headquarters in Langley, Virginia, gave him access to a huge amount of information. The names

They, our agents in the Cold War against the Soviet Union, risked their lives, helped keep you free, and died because this warped, murdering traitor wanted a bigger house and a Jaguar.

—*James Woolsey,* Director of the CIA, speaking about Aldrich Ames

> The most damaging mole in CIA history.
>
> —*Alan Dulles*, referring to Aldrich Ames

of dozens of CIA assets in the Soviet Union and two inside the Soviet Embassy, along with descriptions of more than a hundred operations, were all in the files. For example, Ames learned that Adolf Tolkachev (code name: Vanquish) had provided details about the Soviet military's airpower, and that a recording device in a tunnel beneath Moscow was intercepting top-secret communications from the KGB.

Ames divorced his first wife, but the settlement and Rosario's spending put him in debt. He was fantasizing about robbing a bank when he remembered that the KGB had offered a CIA colleague $50,000 to spy. Ames took a page from the CIA's classified telephone book, underlined his name, and stuck it in an envelope with a note. Then he walked into the Soviet Embassy in Washington and handed the envelope to the guard. (It was addressed to the head of the KGB in Washington.) The message exposed two FBI sources in the embassy. The men were tricked by the KGB into returning to Moscow, were tried, and were executed. On June 13, 1985, Rick Ames volunteered the names of twenty CIA Soviet spies, and several days later five more, including his friend, Fedorenko. He left documents and information at dead drops in various parks in northern Virginia, and retrieved bags of cash from the Soviets.

The bug beneath Moscow stopped working and other covert operations fell apart. When twenty-three CIA Soviet spies in the Soviet Union disappeared, the CIA launched an investigation. Meanwhile, Ames was assigned to Rome. In Italy, he bought custom-made suits, hand-sewn shoes, and a flashy sports car. Friends assumed the money was from Rosario's family in Colombia. They never imagined it arrived in brown shopping bags from Moscow.

In the fall of 1989, Ames paid cash for a $540,000 home outside of Washington. It was a gift, he claimed, from his mother-in-law. The traitor and his wife refurnished it and put a Jaguar in the driveway. To avert suspicion, he borrowed money for the car. Nonetheless, the spending attracted attention from the CIA's mole-hunting team. (Ames was making under $70,000 a year.) For the next few years, Ames and the people who were secretly investigating him passed in the halls and attended meetings together.

BETTY DUVALL

Disguised as a "country girl," Confederate spy Betty Duvall rode out of Washington. When she reached General Bonham, she took out a tucking comb and unwound her hair. Inside, there was a small package wrapped in silk. It contained a ciphered message that described the movements of the Union Army.

On February 21, 1994, twenty-five FBI agents met at a parking lot near the Ames home. The plan was to get Rick out of the house so he couldn't destroy evidence. The spy was arrested driving his fancy Jaguar. When he was pushed into the backseat of an FBI car, he mumbled to himself, "Think, think, think." Rosario was taken into custody minutes later. She left behind dozens of unworn designer dresses, a hundred boxes of panty hose, several hundred pairs of shoes, and a Polaroid photograph of property purchased by the KGB for the Ames's retirement. It was a lovely piece of land on a river outside of Moscow.

Rick Ames was sentenced to life in prison without parole. He promised to divulge everything if Rosario was given a lighter sentence. The less-devoted wife called her husband a "liar and manipulator." Her sentence was sixty-three months, then she was deported. "It was simply how the game was played," Ames explained. He also admitted, "I did it for the money."

Ames being arrested by the FBI

> **[Aldrich Ames] simply told us who were the traitors in our midst. I consider him a very fine fellow.**
>
> —*Viktor Cherkashin,* Ames's KGB handler

OLEG GORDIEVSKY

After Ames told the KGB that General Oleg Gordievsky, the chief of the undercover KGB office in London, was secretly working for MI6, Gordievsky was recalled. While under periodic questioning in Moscow, the British arranged his escape. The spy wrapped himself in a thermal blanket to mask his body heat from a Soviet temperature-scanning device, hid in a British embassy car, and escaped. "He [Ames] has the blood of a dozen officers on his hands," said Gordievsky. "He would have had my blood, too, had I not managed to escape."

ROBERT PHILIP HANSSEN

Robert Philip Hanssen was filling a dead drop in a Virginia park when he was arrested in 2001. For some twenty years, he was a KGB mole inside the FBI. He sold information about U.S. security (including the existence of the tunnel beneath the Soviet Embassy) and betrayed many CIA agents. Hanssen may have decided to become a spy after reading a book by KGB mole Kim Philby.

PLANTING LIES
Misinformation and Propaganda

GOVERNMENTS HAVE USED DECEPTIONS to mislead, confuse, scare, trap, undermine, or weaken enemies for centuries. Imagine George Washington's glee when he learned that the British ships bound for Rhode Island had changed direction after he wrote a fake letter detailing plans to invade New York. Washington also instructed his soldiers to bury the dead late at night in unmarked graves. He wanted the British to think that the Continental Army was invincible.

During the Vietnam War, the U.S. tried to undermine the North Vietnamese by creating an imaginary resistance movement, the "Sacred Sword of the Patriots League." A recruit parachuted into the North, followed by a dozen empty chutes. (The chutes carried large blocks of ice to make them fall as if they were carrying bodies.) The U.S. hoped that the Vietcong would discover the parachutes and conclude that the resistance was huge.

Leaders will also distort information to raise fears with their own citizens in order to strengthen support for an unpopular military action. In the 1930s, the Nazis claimed that the clever Jews were taking all the good jobs in Germany. The propaganda increased anti-Semitism and paved the way for an unbelievable plan: the death camps.

In the late 1980s, Iraqis hid buildings within buildings. They buried facilities underground and disguised water pipes, power lines, and emissions. Normally, a military target would have security fences and guards, so the Iraqis removed them. Missile sites looked like elementary schools from the air. Saddam Hussein hoped that photos taken by spy satellites would confuse the enemy, and later the bombers during the 1990–1991 Gulf War.

Deceptions are dangerous for many reasons. Is the enemy really fooled? If Operation Bodyguard had failed, the Nazis probably would have concentrated their forces in Normandy and killed many more Allied soldiers on the beaches. If Operation Mincemeat hadn't been successful, the Germans and Italians could have trapped the Allies on the island of Sicily. In the sixth century BCE, Sun Tzu wrote a sentence that has been quoted by leaders ever since: "All warfare is based on deception." All spying, too!

> It's not a failure of the CIA. It's a matter of their intelligence being good, our deception being better.
>
> —*G. Balachandran*, Indian scientist, after India exploded a nuclear weapon

TOKYO ROSE

Iva Toguri, an American, was convicted of being Tokyo Rose, the name given to the sultry voice that talked about unfaithful sweethearts and American casualties on Radio Tokyo during World War II. Toguri served six years in prison and was pardoned in 1977. In reality, the voice of "Tokyo Rose" belonged to several women.

BODYGUARD OF LIES

"IN WARTIME," Prime Minister Winston Churchill said, "truth is so precious that she should always be attended by a bodyguard of lies." In the spring of 1944, the most precious truth was the time and location of the Allied invasion of Europe. It was attended by a deception campaign called, appropriately, Operation Bodyguard.

Allied troops would come from England, across the English Channel. There were two sensible places to land on the French coast: Pas de Calais and Normandy. The deception campaigns were designed to convince the Germans that the landing would take place in Pas de Calais. At the same time, Allied forces were preparing to come ashore on the Normandy beaches.

A network of German spies reported a buildup of forces in southeast England, the best spot for a crossing to Pas de Calais. (They were actually double agents working for the British. They called themselves the XX Committee, or Double Cross Committee.) The real troops were in the southwest, closer to Normandy. The Germans picked up endless radio signals from the southeast. The radio traffic was transmitted to indicate that the center of activity was nearer Pas de Calais. Meanwhile, it was very quiet in the southwest.

The Allies also used the ideas of movie set designers to mislead the Nazis. When the German pilots and crews looked down, they saw rows of tanks, planes, and landing crafts. The dummies were constructed of plywood, canvas, and supporting metal rods. One framework that looked just like a Sherman tank could be placed on a jeep and moved across a field.

U.S. General George S. Patton posed as the commander of the imaginary First U.S. Army Group (FUSAG) in southeast England. Obviously, the Germans concluded, the highly respected Patton must be directing the invasion from the southeast. In Geneva, British spies bought all the maps of Pas de Calais. German spies took notice.

As the Allies started across the Channel toward Normandy, Royal Air Force squadrons dropped foil strips near Pas de Calais. The German radar operators heard echoes off the strips and believed they were listening to the sounds of approaching ships. Small motorboats with sound equipment slipped in close to the beaches and played bugle calls, loud commands, anchors dropping, and engines humming. Also, dummy parachutists with firecrackers (guns!), and Special Forces with record players broadcasting the sounds of battle descended from the skies.

On June 1, 1944, the BBC broadcasted the first line of a poem by Paul Verlaine. The words in French meant: "The long sobbing of the violins of autumn." It was a signal that the D-Day invasion was about to begin. The French Underground listened to their radios for the second line of the poem. On June 5, 1944, "Wound my heart with monotonous languor" alerted members of the Resistance to begin their attacks. They blew up railway lines, cut phone wires, and laid ambushes disrupting troop movements and supply lines. On June 6, the Allies landed in Normandy.

MAQUISARD USING TRUCK
A member of the French Resistance
waiting for an unsuspecting German

SOLDIERS LIFTING UP INFLATABLE TANK
Inflatable tanks were used in North Africa and on the continent of Europe to convince German pilots that the enemy was stronger than it really was.

WORLD WAR II
OPERATION CODE NAMES
Bodyguard: the overall campaign to deceive the Nazis about the D-Day landings
Bolero: campaign for the buildup of American troops in Britain
Fortitude: the largest deception in Operation Bodyguard, including Fortitudes North and South
Fortitude North or "Rosebud": campaign in the north (Norway)
Fortitude South or "Quicksilver": campaign in Pas de Calais

Mincemeat: campaign to deceive the Germans and Italians about the invasion from the south (Sicily)
Neptune: campaign to transport troops across the English Channel in 6,939 vessels, and to build a secure beachhead
Overlord: real operation that began on June 6, 1944, the most massive invasion in history
Sea Lion: German plan to invade England (not executed)
Vendetta, Ferdinand, Ironside, Zeppelin: false invasions

The XX Committee alerted Berlin that huge forces remained in southeast England. The "infallible" German spy Cato (British agent Garbo) confirmed that the Normandy invasion was a diversion. The Allies, he said, were planning to send Patton and FUSAG into Pas de Calais with plans to surround the German Army. The powerful German Fifteenth Division remained in Pas de Calais for six weeks waiting for Patton. Meanwhile, the general arrived in Normandy with a real American army. Today, the D-Day invasion is still considered the most massive and successful amphibious landing operation in modern military history.

Always mystify, mislead, and surprise the enemy.

—*General Thomas "Stonewall" Jackson*

When able to attack, we must seem unable; when using our forces, we must seem inactive; when we are near, we must make the enemy believe we are far away; when far away, we must make him believe we are near.

—*Sun Tzu,* The Art of War

IDENTIFICATION PHOTO OF JUAN PUJOL

Juan Pujol (British code name Garbo, German code name Cato) fabricated a spy network of twenty-five agents and contacts. He created a personality, history, and handwriting for each one. The Nazis believed the intelligence provided by the spy ring, but it was all lies. Toward the end of the war, the confused Germans rewarded their spy with the Iron Cross. In England, Garbo became a Member of the British Empire.

OPERATION MINCEMEAT

ON APRIL 30, 1943, a British submarine rose to the surface off the coast of Spain. Minutes later, a dead man was lowered into the sea. He was wearing a life vest and the uniform of the British Royal Marines. "Major William Martin" had many items in his pockets, including letters from his girlfriend, father, and bank manager, and ticket stubs to a recent play in London. He also had a locked briefcase chained to his wrist. The tides and currents nudged the corpse toward the sand.

The body was discovered by a fisherman. When German operatives learned that a dead British officer had washed up on the beach, a man with a locked briefcase chained to his wrist, they were very interested. The briefcase indicated that Martin was a courier transporting top-secret documents. The life vest confirmed that he had gone down in a plane off the coast. The Germans removed the papers from their sealed envelopes, photographed them, replaced them, and resealed the envelopes. Meanwhile, the British contacted Spanish authorities and asked that the corpse be returned. Obviously, the Germans deduced, the courier was very important.

The documents in Martin's briefcase concerned Operation Husky, the code name for the Allied invasion of Europe from the south. Husky was the actual code name for the invasion, in case the Nazis intercepted Allied communications, but everything else was false. A letter in the briefcase reported a

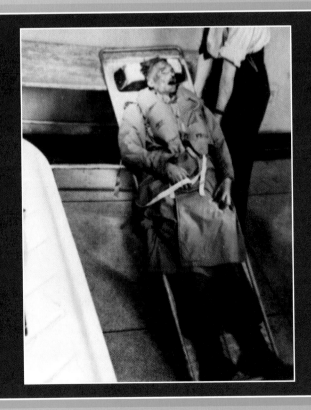

CORPSE OF MAJOR MARTIN
Who was the real Major Martin? His real name (revealed in 2003) was Glyndwr Michael. The thirty-four-year-old man had poisoned himself in a warehouse in London.

AMERICAN TROOPS CARRYING RIFLES THROUGH THE SURF

On June 6, 1944, 73,000 American troops landed in Normandy, along with 61,715 British and 21,400 Canadian soldiers. By June 11, 326,547 troops and 54,186 vehicles had arrived. The total number of casualties on D-Day is estimated at 10,000 (2,500 dead). The Allies' password? Mickey Mouse.

change of plans: The invasion would begin in Greece rather than Italy. It also said that the Allies would try to trick the Germans into thinking that the landing would take place on the island of Sicily, to divert their attention. When the documents arrived in Berlin, German intelligence thought it was a British deception. Hitler, however, was fooled. Two weeks after the body was discovered, it was returned to British officials in Spain. They determined that the envelopes had been opened and resealed. Winston Churchill received a telegram from British intelligence confirming that the operation had been successful. It said simply, "Mincemeat Swallowed Whole."

When the Allies came ashore in Sicily, they were met with just two German divisions and one small Italian unit. Meanwhile, many powerful German units moved into Greece and prepared for an invasion there. The Nazis on the Greek coast stared through their binoculars at the empty horizon and waited for the Allied ships to appear.

OPERATION BERNHARD

AFTER THE GERMANS LOST THE BATTLE OF BRITAIN IN 1940, Hitler had a clever idea: destroy the enemy from within by producing counterfeit money. The plan had two advantages. When the bills were discovered, there would be chaos. No one would know which money was real. Also, the British pounds and American dollars could help pay for the German war effort. The head of the Gestapo didn't like the plan. "Forging money . . . is the sort of thing that will bring the Third Reich into disrepute," he wrote to another officer, but Hitler's idea was implemented.

The top-secret plan was named for its leader, SS Major Bernhard Krueger. The forgers were prisoners in the Sachsenhausen death camp. They included expert engravers, printers, and counterfeiters. To maintain security, the 142 men were isolated. If they became ill, they were shot.

The Nazis purchased the most sophisticated printing and graphic equipment. One of the challenges was to decipher the code behind the serial numbers on the five- and ten-pound notes (paper bills). The counterfeits were printed on pure linen until the Nazis realized that British notes were made of "random rags and corset cuttings." To age the bills, prisoners folded, soiled, and passed them back and forth, over and over again. By 1945, Operation Bernhard had produced 150 million pounds. On February 22, the presses turned out the first hundred dollar bill. Production of a million dollars was scheduled for the next day, but the German high command closed down the operation. It was the end of the war and they wanted to destroy evidence of any wrongdoing. They ordered the presses dismantled and the forgers executed.

Some of the pounds did reach England, but most of them went to pay for the war, including German spies. When British agents found out about the counterfeit five- and ten-pound notes, they alerted the Bank of England. The bank responded by refusing to honor bills greater than one pound. The prisoner forgers escaped, and some who felt Krueger had saved them from certain death came to his defense after the war. Krueger was exonerated and fled to South America.

ELYEZA BAZNA

Elyeza Bazna (code name: Cicero) was a private valet for the British ambassador in Turkey and a German spy. He was well paid for the top-secret information he provided, including the code word "Overlord." The Germans failed to take Overlord seriously, thinking it was too good to be true. Cicero was paid in Operation Bernhard bills, was caught using the money, and imprisoned.

FORGED CURRENCY ISSUED BY GERMAN INTELLIGENCE, CIRCA 1943–44

This counterfeit English bill was issued by German intelligence. Britannia's eyes are a bit dull, her lower lip is too thin, the cross and fleur-de-lis on her crown are not well defined, and the vase and its shadow are a touch light. Otherwise, it is almost perfect.

The Nazis decided that the perfect place to hide the evidence of Operation Bernhard would be the bottom of a lake. Plates, printing presses, and millions of forged British pounds were transported to Lake Toplitz in Austria and dropped overboard. Many years later, professional divers sank into the murky water to see what they could find. In 1963, 1983, and 2000, they came to the surface with handfuls of British pound notes. Many people believe there is Nazi gold down there, too.

63

GIFTS, TUNNELS, AND OTHER CLANDESTINE OPERATIONS

THE OBJECTIVE OF EVERY OPERATION is to gain an advantage. One way to get a step ahead of your enemy is by gathering intelligence. (It may come from spies or from surfing the Internet!) Sometimes the goal is not information; an operation or deception campaign is initiated to gain a military advantage. For example, the purpose of the D-Day operation was to secure a foothold in France with minimal casualties.

The history of espionage includes many seemingly absurd ideas that became successful operations. Imagine the expressions on the faces of the Greek leaders when someone suggested building a horse as big as a mountain. The Trojan Horse was a huge success, because it gave the Greeks a military advantage. The Soviet gift "The Thing" was much smaller, as were its thoughtful presenters, but it was also a triumph. The innovative bug gathered intelligence for six years. (It's enough to make you suspicious of all gifts.) Operation Pastorius failed to provide a military advantage, and Harvey's Hole succeeded in gathering intelligence. Another underground operation, the Cu Chi tunnels, allowed the Vietcong to eavesdrop on the Americans during the Vietnam War.

"THE THING"

BEWARE OF GREEKS BEARING GIFTS . . . and Soviet schoolchildren.

In 1946, adorable schoolchildren presented a gift to Averill Harriman, the U.S. ambassador to Moscow. It was a wooden carving of the Great Seal of the United States. Harriman hung the two-foot-wide seal over his desk. Where else? Little did he know that a bug below the beak of the scowling eagle transmitted conversations to the KGB.

Until the Great Seal bug, no one in Western intelligence had seen a listening device without a power source—either batteries or wires with an electric current. The Russian bug was a "target" device activated by a beam. When it was turned on, it became a microphone. Otherwise, it was almost undetectable. The voices traveled by radio waves to a receiver. Across the street from the embassy, Russians huddled in a parked van and recorded the conversations.

The Great Seal bug was invented in a Siberian labor camp by Leon Theremin. The Soviet scientist is better known for a box with two antennas that he created in 1919. If you wave a hand between the antennas, the box produces hideous and heavenly sounds. The "Theremin" was the first step in the history of electronic music.

"The Thing" was discovered in 1952, but it wasn't revealed to the world until 1960. In the meantime, British intelligence copied Theremin's design and, along with their American allies, planted their imitations and eavesdropped on the Soviets.

Henry Cabot Lodge shows the bug in the Great Seal at the United Nations

THE TROJAN HORSE

IN THE FIRST CENTURY BCE, poets wrote about the siege of a walled city and a wooden horse. Was the story true or just a myth? In the *Iliad*, the saga of the Trojan War began at the royal wedding of Peleus, king of a race of people created from ants, and Thetis, a sea nymph. Eris (goddess of chaos) wasn't invited, because she often caused trouble. She attended anyway, and tossed a golden apple at the guests. The apple was for the fairest of them all, she told them, causing trouble once again! Hera (goddess of marriage), Athena (goddess of wisdom), and Aphrodite (goddess of love) each insisted the apple was meant for herself. They asked Zeus to decide, but he was far too wise. He suggested they seek the answer from Paris, son of the King of Troy.

The goddesses offered Paris bribes: power, glory, or love. Paris chose love and Aphrodite. She promised him the most beautiful woman in the world. Unfortunately, the fairest, Helen, was married to Menelaus, King of Sparta. Paris was undeterred. He traveled to Sparta, befriended the king, met Helen, and eloped. Paris and Helen were married around 1200 BCE in Troy. Of course, Menelaus was furious, and set sail with a thousand ships.

The siege of Troy lasted ten years, because the Greeks couldn't break down the thick walls of the city. Finally, they built a huge horse out of pieces of fir. They rolled it to the gates and sailed away. A Greek spy, Sinon, persuaded the Trojans that the Greeks had given up and left a gift, so the Trojans pulled the enormous horse inside the walls.

In the middle of the night, the Greek ships returned. Soldiers slipped down ropes from the horse's belly and opened the gates. When the Trojans awoke, their city was in flames. Before long, the men were massacred and the women enslaved. Menelaus forgave Helen (she was very beautiful, so easy to forgive) and together they sailed for Sparta.

For centuries, people believed that Troy, the Trojan War, and the Trojan Horse were myths invented by poets. In1871, Heinrich Schliemann, a German businessman, began digging in Turkey. He chose a site based on clues he found in Homer's tale the *Iliad*. Schliemann discovered nine cities, one on top of the other. The seventh, which was destroyed around 1190 BCE, had walls that were sixteen feet thick. Many people believe the businessman found Troy.

The tale of the Trojan Horse has produced several common expressions. A very beautiful woman is said to have "a face that launched a thousand ships." A person, device, or dangerous code in a computer program may be called a "Trojan horse." The most famous saying from the ancient story is a warning: "Beware of Greeks bearing gifts."

Don't trust the horse, you people of Troy. Some trick is concealed here.

—*Virgil*, The Aeneid

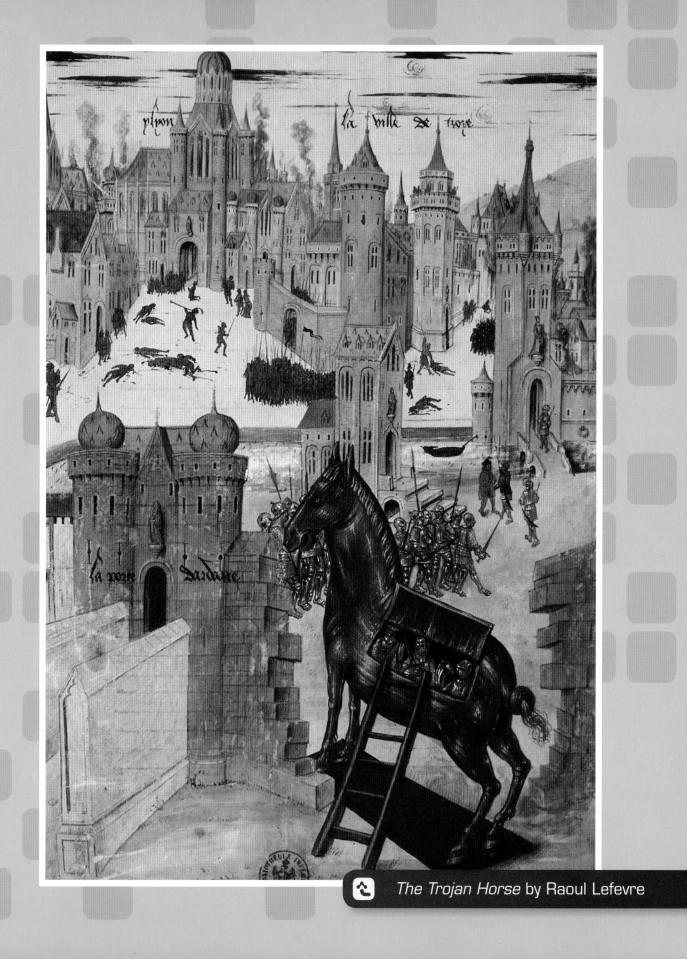

The Trojan Horse by Raoul Lefevre

SPYING FROM BELOW

DURING THE COLD WAR, British and American intelligence agencies started digging underneath East Berlin. Although a nuclear attack would come from the skies, advance warning might come from below. The objective was to tap landlines carrying secret communications. According to *The New York Times*, the FBI tunneled beneath the Soviet Embassy in Washington, D.C., a few decades later. The agency hoped to listen in on conversations in the rooms above, but the operation was exposed by Robert Hanssen, a Russian mole.

Many Vietcong lived in the Cu Chi Tunnel during the Vietnam War. It was actually a maze of 155 miles of tunnels running from Saigon to the Cambodian border. It was so large, there were street signs! Below the ground, the Vietcong bathed, cooked, slept, cared for the sick, sheltered their animals, and occasionally conducted espionage. In one place, the tunnel passed beneath a U.S. military base. American soldiers discussed secret maneuvers, unaware that their enemy may have been listening several feet below.

The North Koreans tunneled under the Demilitarized Zone (DMZ) into South Korea. "One tunnel can be more powerful than ten atomic bombs put together and the tunnels are the most ideal means of penetrating the South's fortified line," said President Kim Il-Song in 1971. The first of four tunnels was discovered in 1974. (There may be twenty-two more.) A group of "Invasion Tunnel Hunters" believed that the Communists were slipping spies into South Korea and planning to use the underground pathways for a future invasion.

It's easy to forget what intelligence consists of: luck and speculation. Here and there a windfall, here and there a scoop.

—*John Le Carré*

We may be likened to scorpions in a bottle, each capable of killing the other, but only at the risk of his own life.

—*J. Robert Oppenheimer,* nuclear scientist

HARVEY'S HOLE

IN THE EARLY 1950s, Americans read a chilling statistic in their morning newspaper: If an atomic bomb were dropped on the U.S., it would kill approximately 36 million people the first day. The British learned that there would be four minutes between the sound of the air-raid siren (giving notice of an incoming bomb) and the explosion. As a result, intelligence agencies in Washington and London became obsessed with getting any information that would give them advance warning of a Soviet attack.

Berlin was on the front line of the Cold War. The German city was divided into four sectors, each one controlled by a different country. Thousands of American, British, French, and Russian spies operated in the shadows. Belowground, miles of landlines carried top-secret coded communications. The code makers and code breakers on both sides were locked in an invisible battle.

In 1952, Bill Harvey from the CIA's Office of Special Operations flew into Berlin. He was an overweight man with a bullfrog voice who often kept a pearl-handled revolver on his desk. Harvey was there to oversee the construction and operation of a tunnel. It would be a joint British/American (SIS/CIA) intelligence operation officially called "Stopwatch Gold." Unofficially, it was "Harvey's Hole."

In 1953, George Blake, a member of the British Intelligence Service, came home a hero. He had been a prisoner in South Korea from 1950 to 1953. As the Salvation Army chorus sang, Blake descended the steps from the ambulance plane in Oxfordshire, England. No one suspected that the thin, bearded man had volunteered to become a Soviet mole. His code name was Diomid (Diamond), because he was brilliant and valuable.

The main operation building for Harvey's Hole was disguised to look like a radar station. It had a deep basement (for the tunnel's three thousand tons of dirt), power generators, barracks, and a large kitchen. Hundreds of sections of six-foot-wide steel tunnel liners were assembled in Virginia and transported by ship and train to Berlin. In the fall of 1954, with Eisenhower and Churchill howling for intelligence, the digging began. The previous January, "the Diamond" had handed a description of Operation Stopwatch Gold to the KGB.

CU CHI TUNNEL

The Cu Chi Tunnel was an underground fortress complete with a theater, printing presses, and water buffalo. The Vietcong booby-trapped entrances with trip wires that released grenades or boxes of scorpions on intruders. Today, Westerners may take a guided tour of some of the tunnels.

BERLIN TUNNEL

A sign was left behind in the tunnel. The words (in German) matched the ones on a sign above: "You are now entering the American sector."

> One of the most valuable and daring projects ever undertaken.
>
> —*Allen Dulles,* CIA, about the Berlin Tunnel

The Berlin tunnel was sixteen feet belowground and just under five hundred yards long. There were narrow-gauge train tracks down the middle for moving equipment, and rows of sandbags on either side for muffling the noise. On March 10, 1955, the engineers reached the Soviet cable inches below the heels of the East German guards. At the same time, Dulles drew up a U.S. reaction in case the tunnel was discovered: "flat, indignant denial."

The Soviets had a problem. Even though they knew about the tunnel, they couldn't shut down the landlines without endangering their well-placed mole. The KGB decided not to alert the Red Army or the GRU. For eleven months and eleven days, the Allies transcribed 443,000 conversations from 50,000 reels of magnetic tape in offices in Berlin, London, and Washington. (At one point, there were more than 300 people in England and 350 in the U.S. transcribing messages.) The SIS/CIA joint operation received a massive amount of intelligence that provided insights into Soviet thinking.

Eventually, the Soviets decided to "accidentally" discover the tunnel. At 12:30 A.M. on April 22,

RUSSIAN SOLDIER REMOVING INSULATION FROM CABLE

Journalists note as Soviet officers point out where the West had tapped into the East German phone system.

1956, a Soviet truck stopped just above the tap. East German soldiers tumbled out and started digging with shovels and pickaxes. When they came to a locked steel door, they dug a hole through a nearby wall and looked into the sophisticated preamplification chamber. One of the soldiers said (in German), "How did they do it? It's fantastic!"

When the tunnel was discovered, a Soviet delegation was in London for the first state visit in decades. Both countries decided to keep quiet about British involvement so as not to disrupt the talks. The "American spy tunnel," said an appalled spokesman for the Red Army, is a "blatant act of imperialist aggression and international gangsterism." The Soviets held press conferences and gave journalists and photographers a guided tour. They hoped to embarrass the West, but the reaction was the opposite. Many Americans felt that World War III was inevitable, and wondered what their government was doing about it. The *Boston Post* reported, "Frankly, we didn't know the American intelligence agents were that smart."

OPERATION PASTORIUS

UNLIKE THE GIFTS AND TUNNELS, Operation Pastorius was a complete failure. In 1942, eight German saboteurs attempted to disrupt the production of ships, tanks, and airplanes in America. J. Edgar Hoover, the head of the FBI, took full credit for rooting out the Nazis, but they were actually betrayed by their leader. In espionage, success and failure can depend on luck.

In the spring of 1942, German tanks, airplanes, and thousands of guns were being destroyed on the Russian front. At the same time, the U.S. was stepping up its production: 60,000 planes, 45,000 tanks, 20,000 antiaircraft guns, and 6 million tons of shipping. Hitler believed that whoever had the most planes, tanks, guns, and ships would win the war. The Nazis decided to sabotage American plants. The operation was called Pastorius.

Eight recruits reported to the German intelligence organization (Abwehr) sabotage school on the shore of Lake Quenz, forty miles from Berlin. The men studied how to blow up bridges, assemble bombs, and write codes in invisible ink. The saboteurs memorized facts about American sports stars, teams, and politics. They sang "The Star Spangled Banner" and "Oh, Susannah" and practiced American slang. "Scram," they said, and "What a bunch of nuts." They were headed to America, and they wanted to sound just like Americans.

Two German U-boats (submarines) left the coast of France in May 1942. Each one carried four Nazi saboteurs. One U-boat was headed for Florida, the other for Long Island, New York. The submarines traveled on the surface until aircraft buzzed overhead, then they dove. The spies got violently seasick.

On June 13, 1942, the first U-boat landed in the fog on Long Island. Not only were the Germans a few miles off target, but they also ran into a U.S. Coast Guard seaman patrolling the beach. "Who are you?" the unarmed seaman yelled. "Fishermen. From Easthampton," the German replied. "Our boat ran aground." The seaman offered to let the men stay in the Coast Guard station until daylight, but the leader of the spies, George Dasch, refused. Instead, he offered the young man a bribe to keep quiet. "I never saw you before in my life," the terrified seaman said before racing down the beach.

The Germans buried their explosives and detonators, changed their clothes, and headed for the local railroad station. Meanwhile, the seaman and other members of the Coast Guard began digging in the sand with their hands. They found the boxes filled with explosives and uniforms with the insignias of the German Navy. Four days later, the second U-boat unloaded four saboteurs in Florida. They came ashore in bathing suits, and no one noticed.

The Nazi plan was to blow up aluminum plants and railway lines to disrupt the war production. The saboteurs might have been successful and the loss could have affected the outcome of the war, but Dasch never intended to go through with it. "You'll be reading about me in all the papers pretty soon," he told an old friend in New York. Dasch called the FBI and demanded to talk to the director, J. Edgar Hoover. The agency thought it was a crank call.

Supplies hidden by the saboteurs: TNT, blasting caps, and $200,000 in cash

No one knows why Dasch became a traitor. Was he convinced the saboteurs would be caught after the slipup on the beach? Did he resent the Nazis for not giving him a more important role in the party? Did he want to be an American hero? Or did he simply want to save his own skin? Dasch convinced one of his men to give up, too, but insisted he stay in New York to watch the others. Meanwhile the leader of Operation Pastorius took a train to Washington, D.C., and turned himself in at FBI headquarters. When he realized that he wasn't going to be a hero, Dasch asked to be jailed with the other spies so no one would know he was the traitor.

The New York Times reported that FBI agents pursued the Germans "almost from the moment the first group set foot on United States soil" and that they had seized enough equipment for "a two-year campaign of terror." Dasch and his accomplice were imprisoned. The other six were tried and electrocuted on August 8, 1942. Three years after the war ended, the two traitors were released from Leavenworth Prison and deported to Germany.

BANG!

Weapons, Detonators, Bombs, and Detection Devices

ESPIONAGE AND WARFARE have produced many imaginative and gruesome weapons. In the ancient world, poison was a popular choice. It was called the "coward's weapon," because it was almost risk-free for the perpetrator. In 1915, a German spy in Washington, D.C., experimented with deadly germs. Anton Dilger grew strains of anthrax and glanders cultures in his basement, dubbed "Tony's Lab." He paid dockworkers in Virginia, Maryland, and New York to infect animals that were being shipped to American soldiers in Europe. (In 1918, Dilger caught a deadly germ and died of influenza.)

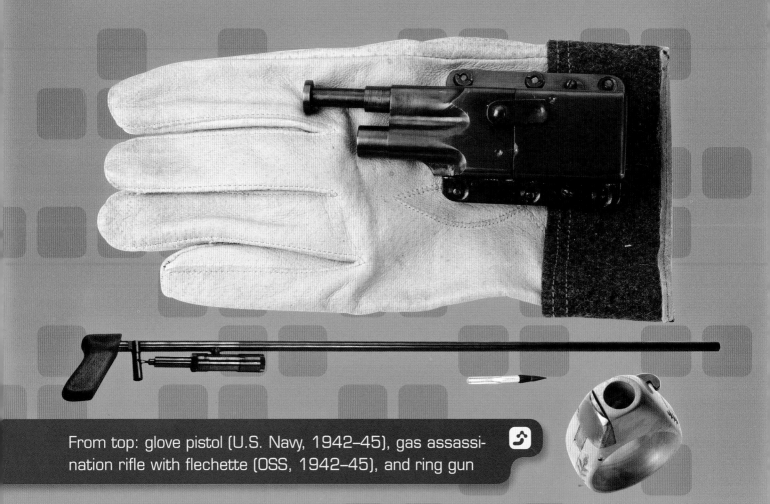

From top: glove pistol (U.S. Navy, 1942–45), gas assassination rifle with flechette (OSS, 1942–45), and ring gun

Clockwise from top left: liberator pistol, tear gas pen (CIA, 1948), double switchblade, assassination weapon in cigarette pack (KGB, 1950s), and lipstick pistol (KGB, 1965).

KGB assassins sometimes used a pen filled with lethal gas (hydrocyanic acid). Thirty minutes before the killing, the spy swallowed an antidote pill in case he or she inhaled the gas by mistake.

[We] did everything from plotting ways to poison the capital's water systems to drawing up assassination plans for U.S. leaders.

—*Oleg Kalugin*

Clockwise from top left: Cigarette case gun (NKVD, 1939), tobacco pipe pistol (British, 1939–45), photo of Black Tom Island, fighting knife with scabbard (OSS, 1943–45), and flashlight gun

During [President] Wilson's border war with Mexican bandits in 1916, the U.S. Army hired four Mexican citizens to poison revolutionary leader Francisco "Pancho" Villa. The operatives were instructed by a member of General John Pershing's staff to drop poison tablets in Villa's coffee, but the attempt failed.

—*Stephen Knott*

During World War I, thousands of tons of munitions were stored on a spit of land in New York Harbor. It was an inviting target for German saboteurs. On July 30, 1916, Black Tom Island erupted. Windows in New York City shattered and the Brooklyn Bridge swayed back and forth. The Statue of Liberty was bombarded with fragments, and the explosions were heard one hundred miles away.

In World War II, SOE spies left rubber rats filled with explosives in German storehouses. Dynamite was also disguised as coal and slipped into an enemy's dump. When the explosive was shoveled into the boiler of a train or factory—BANG! Cigars and cigarettes were also deadly. A captured spy could request one last smoke. As it was being lit, he could pull a string with his teeth and shoot a Nazi within a three-foot range.

The oddest way of undermining an enemy is stench warfare. "Who Me," designed by the OSS, was used by the French Resistance in World War II. The compound, which smelled like fecal matter, was sprayed onto Nazi officers in Paris. It was used for just two weeks, because the Maquisards (members of the Resistance) ended up smelling just like the Nazis. (The Pentagon is still experimenting with stench warfare as a way of controlling hostile mobs and enemy troops.)

From 1944 to 1945, the Japanese launched six thousand balloons. They floated aimlessly across the Pacific, riding the trade winds. The balloons carried incendiary devices designed to start forest fires. The attacks were supposed to frighten Americans and erode support for the war. Three hundred and sixty-nine balloons reached the west coast of the United States, and one killed a family of seven. At the same time, the Allies were working on the most destructive weapon of all time.

BULGARIAN UMBRELLA (KGB, 1978)
In September 1978, Georgi Markov, a Bulgarian writer, was murdered on Waterloo Bridge in London. Markov felt a sharp stab in his thigh. When he turned around, he saw a man picking up an umbrella. A pellet fired from the umbrella was filled with ricin—a poison that killed the writer three days later. (The "hit" was ordered by the Bulgarian secret service.)

MANHATTAN PROJECT

IN THE LATE 1930s, U.S. scientists believed that German researchers were developing a weapon of mass destruction. They asked renowned physicist Albert Einstein to pressure President Roosevelt to begin research on a similar weapon. If the two countries ended up in a global war, the one with "the bomb" would have an enormous advantage. In August 1939, Einstein wrote to the president.

The Manhattan Project began in 1942. It took place in secret communities in Tennessee, Washington, New Mexico, and beneath an athletic field in Chicago, Illinois. Many of the participants were immigrants from Europe who had no doubts about Hitler's lust for power and an atomic weapon. The others were American engineers, physicians, and university researchers.

In top-secret labs, the scientists and researchers manipulated radioactive materials. Hospital patients were secretly injected with plutonium to learn the impact of radioactivity on the human body. Radiosodium was poured into a garden sprinkler and sprayed on an alfalfa field to study the effect of radioactive pollution on the environment. Under Stagg Field at the University of Chicago, the scientists produced a controlled nuclear reaction in a squash court. At Los Alamos, New Mexico, J. Robert Oppenheimer and his team created the first nuclear weapons. Gadget, Little Boy, and Fat Man were the silly names given to the deadly bombs.

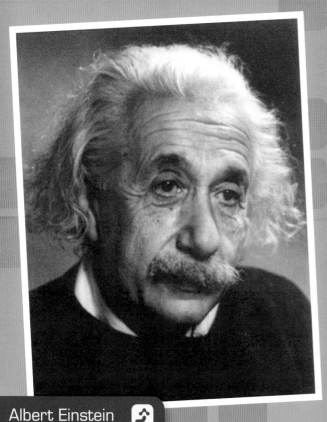

Albert Einstein

In 1945, Little Boy was dropped on Hiroshima, Japan, and Fat Man on Nagasaki. (Gadget was a test.) The results were horrific. Japan surrendered immediately. Many people believe that "the bomb" should never have been used. Was it necessary? The U.S. avoided having to invade Japan, so many American lives were saved, but Little Boy and Fat Man opened the door to a frightening new world.

The U.S. feared that Nazi scientists were developing an atomic weapon, but they never did. However, a number of Los Alamos scientists who were sympathetic to the Soviet Union leaked information to the Russians. Atomic secrets passed through the hands of Julius Rosenberg. Although the Rosenbergs (his wife, Ethel, was part of the spy ring) were arrested and executed in the electric chair, it was too late. The Soviets exploded an atomic bomb similar to Fat Man in 1949, and the Cold War heated up.

Nuclear testing at Los Alamos

Los Alamos bomb tower

I know not with what weapons World War III will be fought, but World War IV will be fought with sticks and stones.

—*Albert Einstein*

JULIUS AND ETHEL ROSENBERG

After Julius Rosenberg was sentenced, he said, "This death sentence is not surprising. It had to be." David Greenglass (Ethel Rosenberg's brother) and his wife were also a part of the Rosenberg spy ring.

ONE OF THE VENONA PAPERS

Many people believed the Rosenbergs were innocent. When the Venona papers (deciphered KGB cables) were released in 1996, they proved otherwise.

<del>TOP SECRET</del>

June 27, 1950

STUDY OF CODE NAMES IN MGB COMMUNICATIONS

Reference is made to the memorandum dated June 23, 1950, bearing the above caption.

Since the referenced memorandum was prepared it has been determined that one JULIUS ROSENBERG is probably identical with the individual described as ANTENNA and LIBERAL in that memorandum. It is also believed now that DAVID GREENGLASS is identical with the individual described as KALIBR, and that RUTH PRINTZ GREENGLASS is identical with the individual known under the code name OSA.

From the information available to date it is believed that ANATOLI ANTONOVICH YAKOVLEV is identical with the individual described under the code name ALEKSEY in the referenced memorandum.

More complete details concerning these individuals will be furnished to you at a later date.

DECLASSIFIED BY
ON 2-30-96 Speckman

A weapon is an enemy even to its owner.

—*Turkish proverb*

FOREST FREDERICK YEO-THOMAS

FOREST FREDERICK YEO-THOMAS was British, but he grew up in France. At the beginning of World War I, "Tommy" was sixteen years old. Despite his father's objections, he became a dispatch rider carrying messages for the U.S. Army on his motorbike. Three years later, he joined the Poles to fight the Bolsheviks. He was captured and sentenced to death. The night before his execution, Yeo-Thomas strangled the guard and fled. It was the first of many escapes for the man who would be known as the "White Rabbit."

Yeo-Thomas was also known as Shelley.

Between the wars, Yeo-Thomas joined a women's fashion house in Paris. Although he was in his forties when World War II broke out, he became a wing commander in the British Royal Air Force and an SOE agent. In 1943, Yeo-Thomas parachuted into France. With two others, he organized resistance groups and created a secret army for operations after the D-Day invasion. The White Rabbit narrowly escaped from the Nazis six times, once by hiding in a hearse.

Shortly after Yeo-Thomas parachuted into France for the last time (February 1944), he was betrayed and arrested. The Nazis wrapped him in chains and lowered him headfirst into ice-cold water. The SOE agent got blood poisoning from the chains and nearly lost his left arm. In Fresnes Prison, Yeo-Thomas spent four months in solitary confinement and three weeks in the dark with little food. The interrogators promised him freedom for a little information, but he revealed nothing. When a German officer ordered the weakened prisoner to stand, Yeo-Thomas said that he only stood for his superiors.

In July and August 1944, the White Rabbit tried to escape two more times. At the Nazi Buchenwald concentration camp, Yeo-Thomas and two others exchanged identities with three dying Frenchmen. As a result, they were transferred and their lives were saved. Yeo-Thomas tried two more escapes in the spring of 1945. He collapsed in the woods and ordered the others to go on without him. The prisoners picked him up, and together they stumbled across a minefield to the American forces.

After the war, the fearless SOE agent received the George Cross, the Military Cross and Bar, the Polish Cross of Merit, and other awards. He testified against war criminals at the Nuremberg Trials, and then returned to his Parisian fashion house. In 1948, Yeo-Thomas retired because of poor health. He lived for another sixteen years, but never recovered from the Nazi beatings and starvation.

THE GETAWAY

IN 1776, JOHN HONEYMAN allowed himself to be caught by soldiers in the Continental Army. He was taken to George Washington and interrogated. Honeyman had been hired by the British to spy, but he was a double agent. He told General Washington where he could find and surprise the British troops. Washington ordered the "spy" locked in the guardhouse, so that no one would know he was a double agent. Later that night a haystack burst into flames. Honeyman's guard rushed off to see what was happening. Mysteriously, the guardhouse was unlocked and the prisoner escaped. Not all escapes are so easy.

Harriet Tubman hid in a potato hole covered with dirt. Virginia Hall limped over the frozen Pyrenees on a wooden leg. Allied soldiers tunneled out of Nazi prisoner-of-war camps, and Oleg Gordievsky rode to safety wrapped in a thermal blanket. Imagine today's spies sitting in an overlit room discussing escape. They would pay close attention.

It is not heroes that make history, but history that makes heroes.

—*Joseph Stalin*

WELBIKE

This folding motorcycle called a Welbike was designed by the SOE for use during World War II. The bike fit inside a fifteen-inch cylinder, which could be tossed out of a plane with a parachute. The paratrooper was supposed to remove the motorcycle and "be mobile within 11 seconds." The bikes were not used extensively by the paratroopers, but were used by soldiers on D-Day. The same company in Welwyn, England, produced the Welrod, a pistol, and the Welsub, a one-man submarine.

Clockwise from top left: Escape map kit, escape boots (Pilots wore these boots in case they were shot down. Behind enemy lines they could remove the tops and blend in with civilians.), escape knife, and escape belt buckle

I conveniently died of typhus on October 13, 1944, after getting into the "guinea pig" block, and changed my identity to that of a Frenchman named Choquet.

—*Frederick Yeo-Thomas*

NOT SO FAST
Brass Knuckles, Suicide Pills, and Retributions

If grisly stories make you queasy, skip to "Blunders" on page 90 immediately. No one will ever know.

MANY SPIES AREN'T AS LUCKY as the White Rabbit. They don't escape. Sometimes, they carry a suicide pill (L-pill). It can be hidden almost anywhere. A captured spy asks for his eyeglasses so he can read his confession. (He probably didn't write it.) He sticks the arm of the glasses in his mouth, chews, and falls dead. Or, perhaps, a doomed woman wants to use the expensive pen in her jacket to sign her name. She bites off the end and closes her eyes. A suicide pill doesn't sound comforting unless the alternative is torture or a painful death.

Suspected spies have faced torture for centuries. Physical and mental abuse are often administered in an attempt to gain information, but the goal isn't always intelligence. Spies are tortured (and killed) as retribution or so that others will be less tempted to spy. (Penkovsky's death may have been filmed by the KGB to dissuade intelligence recruits from betraying their country.) Perhaps the worst retribution occurred in Lidice, Czechoslovakia. When Reinhard Heydrich, a Gestapo general called the "Blond Beast," was assassinated by the SOE, the Nazis killed every man in Lidice, deported every woman to concentration camps, and sent the children to the gas chambers. Five thousand people died.

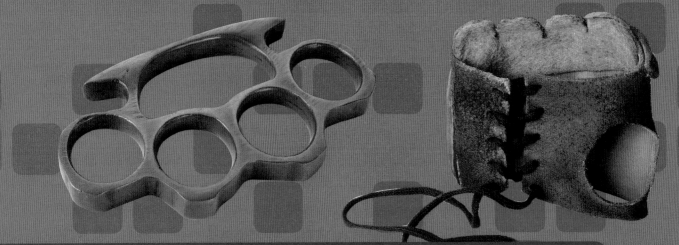

Brass knuckles (British Special Forces, 1939–47), interrogation glove

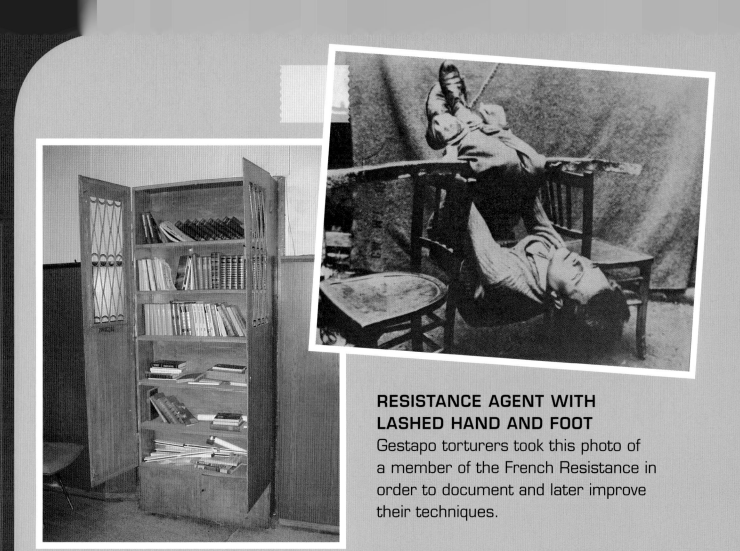

RESISTANCE AGENT WITH LASHED HAND AND FOOT

Gestapo torturers took this photo of a member of the French Resistance in order to document and later improve their techniques.

BUTYRKA PRISON

When a spy was dragged into an interrogator's office in Moscow, he probably didn't suspect what lay behind the cabinet. Stairs! They led to the infamous Butyrka Prison below, where lucky prisoners were quickly executed and unlucky prisoners were held under inhumane conditions for years.

Make the skipper speak, and I even give you authority to promise him his pardon if he gives information; and if he should seem to hesitate, you can go so far as to follow the custom as to men suspected of being spies, and squeeze his thumbs in the hammer of a musket.

—*Napoleon*

OLEG PENKOVSKY

"I ASK YOU TO CONSIDER ME YOUR SOLDIER," Oleg Penkovsky wrote to Queen Elizabeth II and President Kennedy in 1960. "Henceforth the ranks of your Armed Forces are increased by one man." The Soviet colonel provided documents about the Soviet Union's military intentions and capabilities that helped the West avert a nuclear war during the Berlin Crisis (1961) and the Cuban Missile Crisis (1962). President Kennedy used the information to identify and confirm the existence and capabilities of the missiles in Cuba, to anticipate Soviet intentions, and to get international support for a blockade of the island. One author called Penkovsky "the spy who saved the world." In 1963, he was caught, tried, and "shot for treason to the Motherland."

> I don't know of any single instance where intelligence was more immediately valuable than at this time.
>
> —*Richard Helms*, CIA head, speaking about the material provided by Penkovsky ("Penkovsky Papers")

OLEG PENKOVSKY
Oleg Penkovsky was motivated by fear of nuclear war and disillusionment with the closed Soviet system. One of his code names was Hero.

LARRY WU-TAI CHIN

FROM 1952 TO 1981, Larry Wu-Tai Chin was a Chinese language translator for the Foreign Broadcast Information Service (FBIS), a division of the CIA. The Chinese mole provided names of CIA spies in China and anti-Communist Chinese in Korea, and sold national intelligence estimates and analyses to China. His treachery undoubtedly benefited the North Vietnamese during the war and "delayed the end of the Korean War for more than a year."

Chin took many polygraph tests as he advanced in the CIA, and passed every one. He was exposed by Yu Qiangsheng, a Chinese intelligence officer who defected to the U.S. in 1985.

Two weeks after his conviction, Chin put a trash bag over his head, tied it with a shoelace, lay down, crossed his arms, and suffocated.

More people lost their lives because of his [Chin's] treachery than [because of] Aldrich Ames and Robert Hanssen.

—*I. C. Smith*, former FBI Special Agent

CHIN UNDER ARREST
Chin claimed his motivation for spying was to improve relations between China and the United States. He received a million dollars from the Chinese government.

EYEGLASSES WITH CONCEALED CYANIDE PILL (CIA, 1975–77)

If a CIA spy was caught and facing torture, he or she could chew on the arm of these eyeglasses and commit suicide.

Initially it was considered improper to employ women in (SOE) operations. . . . Churchill was asked to adjudicate and deferred on the side of reality. Of the fifty-two female agents sent by SOE into France, seventeen were arrested, of whom twelve died in concentration camps.

—*Mark Lloyd*, Guinness Book of Espionage

VIOLETTE SZABO (1921–1945)

Because of her fluency in French, Violette Szabo was approached by the SOE. She joined FANY (First Aid Nursing Yeomanry) and, like many female SOE agents, used it as a cover. After she parachuted into France the second time, Szabo became involved in a gun battle covering the leader of the French Resistance. (She was supposed to be the best shot in the SOE.) When she ran out of ammunition, she was caught, tortured, and sent to a concentration camp. She was twenty-three years old when she was executed with two other female SOE agents.

ELI COHEN

ELI COHEN was an Egyptian-born Jew whose parents had emigrated from Syria. At Farouk University, he was connected to a young Zionist (pro-Israel) movement. He was expelled from the university in 1949 for his pro-Israel activities, along with all other Jewish students.

When Cohen was twenty-nine, he joined the Israeli intelligence service (Mossad). As part of his training, he learned how to use a variety of weapons and how to handle radio transmissions and cryptography. He also learned "high-speed evasive driving techniques."

In 1961, Cohen traveled to South America and posed as a rich Syrian businessman. In Buenos Aires, Argentina, he befriended politicians and diplomats connected with the Syrian Embassy. A year later, he emigrated to Damascus, Syria, and infiltrated the Ba'ath Party.

For the next four years, Cohen lived in his villa overlooking the Syrian Army headquarters. The dashing spy gave elegant parties entertaining the president and head of intelligence. They reciprocated by inviting him to tour the front lines along the Golan Heights. (At the time, the Syrians controlled the Golan Heights, the source of most of Israel's water. Jewish settlements in the valley below were often targeted by Syrian guns and mortars.)

Cohen suggested planting protective trees around Arab guard posts and bases. Once this was implemented, the Israeli Air Force used the trees to pinpoint and destroy most of the bases. Cohen also provided photos and drawings of fortifications on the Golan Heights and details of Syrian invasion plans. The intelligence helped Israel win the Six Day War in June 1967.

Eventually, Cohen got sloppy, using his radio equipment to send messages to his family. Syrian intelligence tracked him down and arrested him. Despite the pleas of Pope Paul VI and the heads of several governments, "Israel's greatest spy" was hanged in Al Marjeh (Martyr's) Square in Damascus. Forty years later (2005), Cohen's family is still trying to get the spy's body returned to Israel for a proper burial. So far, Syrian President Basha Al-Assad has refused.

Eli Cohen (left) and two other unidentified co-defendants on trial in Damascus, ten days before his execution

BLUNDERS

THE BOOK YOU'RE HOLDING could have been entitled *Failures and Successes*. Every spy story is a failure and a success. If an intelligence agency fails to anticipate an attack or is fooled by a cagey mole, somewhere else, glasses are clinking together in celebration. For example, the Germans believed the D-Day deceptions. What a mistake for them, but what a success for the Allies! The next few pages describe a few blunders from just one point of view.

In the late nineteenth century, Captain Alfred Dreyfus was convicted of espionage and spent twelve years in a penal colony off the coast of South America. It was a terrible mistake, because he was innocent, but the French Army thought the conviction was a huge success. When the injustice was exposed, Dreyfus was eventually freed. French citizens realized the evil of prejudice and the corruption in the military. The Dreyfus Affair prompted legislation to separate the powerful church from the business of the state. A mistake can produce a success.

The Cambridge Spies stole secrets, caused the deaths of many agents, and influenced decisions and policy. They also damaged the bond between two nations, America and Britain. The allies had

SCALE MODEL OF PEARL HARBOR
The Japanese used scale models of Pearl Harbor to plan
their attack on the Pacific fleet on December 7, 1941.

DUSKO POPOV WITH WIFE

Dusko Popov (code name: Tricycle) was a German agent who had volunteered to work for the British (a classic double agent). In August 1941, he arrived in the U.S. with instructions from Germany's Japanese allies concealed in microdots on a fake telegram. Popov was supposed to obtain information on a range of subjects, including Pearl Harbor, and make drawings of military facilities there. Popov showed J. Edgar Hoover the microdots, which included a four-page questionnaire. The FBI director sent a brief memo to President Roosevelt, but didn't mention details relating to Pearl Harbor.

depended upon each other and benefited from an open, trusting relationship since World War II. When the spies were exposed, the U.S. intelligence agencies feared they had been penetrated by British moles. Convinced that there were still more, the suspicious agencies undertook mole hunts for years, ruining many careers in the process. It was a disaster for the West, but what could be better from the KGB's point of view?

The horrific attacks of December 7, 1941, (Pearl Harbor) and September 11, 2001, (World Trade Center and the Pentagon) have a lot in common. America was vulnerable because the government was overconfident and failed to imagine that their enemies would attack the way they did. In both cases, spies traveled to the targets to gather intelligence, and the ugly puzzle made perfect sense afterward. The Japanese chose a target that would give them a military advantage: the Pacific fleet of the U.S. Navy. Osama bin Laden's choice was more symbolic. The World Trade Center represented financial power, and the Pentagon represented military power. The failures forced changes in legislation just as they had in nineteenth-century France.

THE DREYFUS AFFAIR

IN 1894, LETTERS CONTAINING FRENCH MILITARY SECRETS were discovered in the wastebasket of a German military attaché. At the time, the military courts were corrupt and anti-Semitic. Circumstantial evidence pointed to Alfred Dreyfus, a Jewish captain in the French Army. Although his handwriting proved that he was innocent, he was accused of treason. Dreyfus was convicted and sentenced to life imprisonment on Devil's Island.

The Dreyfus Affair polarized France. The political right, the Catholic Church, and *La Libre Parole* (a right-wing newspaper) used the verdict as an excuse to increase their attacks on Jews. Dreyfus's behavior, said the anti-Semites, was proof of Jewish treachery. Others believed that the captain was innocent.

Two years after the conviction, Lieutenant Colonel George Picquart became chief of army intelligence. Although he was openly anti-Semitic, he believed that Dreyfus was innocent and that the well-connected Major Ferdinand Walsin Esterhazy was the real traitor. When Picquart tried to reopen the case, he was transferred to Africa. The French Army was more concerned with their image than with justice.

One morning, the headline in the French newspaper was J'ACCUSE! which means "I accuse!" Well-known novelist Emile Zola accused the military of prejudice. (Zola was convicted of libel and sentenced to imprisonment. He fled to England, but returned when he was granted amnesty.) The political right and the Catholic Church declared that the Dreyfus case was a Jewish conspiracy to destroy the French Army and France. In 1899, the military court conducted a second trial, but the verdict was the same.

Finally, Dreyfus, who had always believed in the army, was pardoned by the French president. The captain was reinstated in 1906 and retired a year later, but returned to his unit to serve his country during World War I. One hundred and one years later, General Jean-Louis Mourrut, head of the French Army's historical service, acknowledged publicly for the first time that the army had been wrong.

JOSEPH McCARTHY

In 1950, Senator Joseph McCarthy claimed that the State Department was "infested" with communists. His accusations prompted an investigation by the House Un-American Activities Committee (HUAC). At public hearings, actors, writers, politicians, and government officials were asked to reveal names. No real spies were identified by McCarthy's crusade, but the careers and lives of many innocent people were ruined.

Dreyfus on trial

Abuse a man unjustly and you will make friends for him.

—*Edgar Watson Howe*

TAKEO YOSHIKAWA

Takeo Yoshikawa was Japan's chief spy in Hawaii prior to Pearl Harbor. He worked under the cover of a vice consul named Morimura. Although there were approximately one hundred and sixty thousand people of Japanese ancestry in Hawaii, Yoshikawa said, "Those men of influence and character who might have assisted me in my secret mission were unanimously uncooperative." The Japanese spy relayed information about U.S. warships and Pearl Harbor.

THE CAMBRIDGE SPIES

IN THE 1930s, five young Englishmen were recruited by Soviet intelligence. Four were undergraduates or recent graduates of Cambridge University, and the fifth was a tutor. The Cambridge spies believed in Soviet-sponsored communism—the political and economic theories of Karl Marx, which advocated the overthrow of capitalism and the establishment of a classless society. They spied because of their beliefs, and refused payment. For several decades, the Cambridge Spy Ring did tremendous damage to Western (British and American) intelligence. There are many conflicting versions of their story—after all, spies are not known for their honesty. The following account is one possibility.

Anthony Blunt was an elegant French tutor and art historian. Kim Philby was the son of a British adventurer and diplomat. He was charming and stylish, but he had a lifelong stammer. The clean-cut Donald Maclean was the son of a member of Parliament and a secretary of education. Guy Burgess, whose father was a Royal Navy officer, was a handsome homosexual. (His code name, Mädchen, is German for girl.) John Cairncross's background was the least privileged. His fellow spies described him as simple and very trusting.

During World War II, the ambitious young men infiltrated the British intelligence agencies and the Foreign Office. Blunt became an officer in MI5. Philby was in the counterespionage section of MI6 and worked closely with SOE. In 1944, he became head of the anti-Soviet section of MI6 responsible for finding Soviet spies and running operations against his secret employer. Maclean was in the Foreign Office, and Burgess was affiliated with MI6 and SOE. John Cairncross was the private secretary to the minister responsible for intelligence services. In 1943, he was posted to MI6 along with Philby. Volumes of information were leaked to the Soviets. They should have been chuckling with delight.

When KGB files became public after the Cold War, they revealed that powerful members of the intelligence organization suspected that the Cambridge spies were double agents who were really loyal to England and were providing misinformation fed by British intelligence. The KGB asked Philby and Blunt to identify British recruits in Moscow. When both men said there were none, the Soviets concluded that the Brits were part of a conspiracy to infiltrate the Russian intelligence organization. (They suspected MI5 and MI6 of doing exactly what the KGB was doing.) But everyone in Moscow played along and even acted on some of the intelligence in case the well-placed moles were genuine.

In 1944, the infection spread to the United States. Maclean became first secretary at the British Embassy in Washington, D.C. His position gave him access to British–U.S. policy on atomic energy, information about nuclear weapons, and details about U.S. military units overseas. Philby arrived in Washington in 1949 and became the liaison between MI6 and the CIA and FBI. The next year, Burgess joined Maclean as second secretary in the British Embassy. When the Americans broke a Soviet code, intelligence analysts realized that someone was leaking nuclear secrets. Philby was informed, and tipped off Maclean through Burgess. Three days before Maclean was to be interrogated, he and Burgess disappeared with Blunt's assistance. The two spies resurfaced years later in Moscow.

Kim Philby, Guy Burgess, and Donald Maclean

Donald Maclean, Guy Burgess, Kim Philby, Anthony Blunt, John Cairncross, and their hangers-on were elegant young men of good family, educated at expensive schools and leading colleges, who had been seduced by the warped logic of Marxism. . . . The Cambridge spies were not only traitors; they were also, in different but closely similar ways, monsters of egotism.

—*John Keegan*

Cairncross was implicated and forced to resign. Philby officially resigned in 1951, but continued to be loosely affiliated with MI6, then followed the other spies to Moscow. In 1964, British intelligence confronted Blunt. The distinguished art historian who had been knighted by the queen revealed significant details about KGB espionage activities, and was not prosecuted at the time. (It would have been embarrassing to admit that Sir Anthony Blunt was a Soviet spy.) When his treachery became public fifteen years later, he was merely stripped of his knighthood.

The Cambridge spies were publicly unmasked, but never prosecuted. For years, Burgess wore the tie from his English boarding school in Moscow. When Maclean died, his ashes were buried next to a memorial honoring his father's service to England. During World War II, Philby had received the Order of the British Empire for his service to Britain. After his defection, he was given the Order of the Red Banner for service to the Soviet Union. The grateful Soviets even put his face on a postage stamp. Imagine all the Russians who slapped him on an envelope.

LYING LADIES, WRITERS, AND CELEBRITIES

MANY GREAT SPIES HAVE BEEN WOMEN. In the past, they had two advantages. Men were less suspicious of the "weaker" sex, and more vulnerable to their charms. (Today, men are still vulnerable, but most understand that women are not weak.) With a sweet smile, a meaningful gaze, a flirtatious turn of a shoulder, or perhaps more, female spies have coaxed secrets out of men for centuries. Of course, charm and seduction weren't their only weapons. (Harriet Tubman didn't bother with either.) The lying ladies also used instinct, intelligence, and courage to achieve their goals.

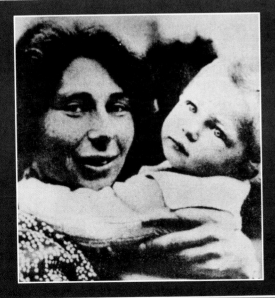

URSULA KUCZYNSKI (1907–2000)
Ursula Ruth Kuczynski (code name: Sonia) was one of the most successful female spies in history. During her twenty-year career (1930–1950) in China and Europe, "Sonia" trained agents, sent radio transmissions, and passed secrets about the atomic bomb to the Soviets. When the GRU ordered her to divorce her husband and marry a British citizen, she did.

BELLE BOYD

BELLE BOYD had shiny blue eyes, sweeping gestures, and "perhaps the best pair of legs in the Confederacy." An interesting observation when you consider that women wore petticoats and skirts to the ground at the time. Boyd dressed in rich colors, reds and greens, and put feathers in her hat. When a drunken Union soldier tried to raise the American flag over her house, she shot him.

The outspoken Virginian was nineteen when she became a Confederate spy. In the spring of 1862, she enchanted Union soldiers and gathered valuable information for General "Stonewall" Jackson and others. By twenty-one, Boyd had been arrested twice. Although she was obviously guilty, she batted her eyelashes and was released. After the war, she had a stage career in England and published a book, *Belle Boyd in Camp and Prison*.

ROSE O'NEAL GREENHOW (1817–1864)
"Wild Rose" O'Neal Greenhow was a renowned rebel spy during the Civil War. She is credited with providing intelligence that enabled the Confederacy to win the battles of Bull Run and Manassas. She continued to get messages to the Confederate generals from her prison cell.

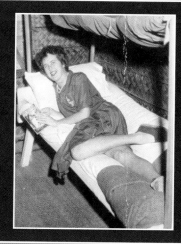

JULIA CHILD (1912–2004)
After the bombing of Pearl Harbor, Julia Child joined the OSS in Washington, D.C. She helped develop a shark repellent, a necessity for sabotage operations against German submarines. Child also worked for the OSS in China and Ceylon, where she met her husband, an OSS officer. "I was not a spy," she insisted, "only a lowly file clerk." Later, Julia Child became a famous chef and star of the first television series on cooking, *The French Chef* (1962–1973).

PAULINE CUSHMAN

IN 1862, a beautiful actress on another stage was offered $300 to toast the President of the Confederacy. Pauline Cushman lifted her glass to Jefferson Davis and was fired by the theater for being a Southern sympathizer. A federal provost marshal realized that the publicity about the actress's toast would make her above suspicion, and help her gain access to Confederate camps.

Cushman charmed her way from one rebel camp to the next. She pretended to be looking for her brother as she gathered information about troop movements and strategies. The Union spy was caught and convicted. Three days before her scheduled hanging, the Confederate troops moved on and left her behind. The actress was rescued by the Yankees and later made an honorary major by President Lincoln.

Pauline Cushman was too well known to continue spying, so she returned to the stage. Dressed in a soldier's jacket, she described her adventures behind enemy lines to audiences across the country. The spy was sixty when she died of an opium overdose (rumored to be intentional). At the time, she was working as a scrubwoman in San Francisco.

I have seen too much not to know that the impression of a woman may be more valuable than the conclusion of an analytical reasoner.

—*Sherlock Holmes*

ELIZABETH BENTLEY
In 1941, Elizabeth Bentley (KGB code name: Clever Girl) was a courier for her lover, a senior Soviet intelligence officer. Bentley stuffed memos into her knitting bag and met contacts at a Washington, D.C., drugstore and in darkened movie theaters. After her lover died, the "Red spy queen" went to the FBI and revealed the names of more than fifty people who were spying in the U.S., including Soviet spymasters and American government officials.

MATA HARI

WHEN MATA HARI faced a firing squad, she was dressed in a floppy black hat with a black ribbon, a black velvet fur-trimmed cape, black kid gloves, and black silk stockings. The tall Dutch woman (she was almost six feet) refused to be blindfolded, waved away the priest, and blew kisses to her twelve executioners.

During World War I, Mata Hari (her name means "Eye of Dawn") requested permission from the French government to visit a lover in a hospital in Germany. The officials agreed, but offered her 1 million francs to spy for them. Before she could get to Germany, she was detained in England and questioned. "Very well," she said, "then I am going to make a confession to you. I am a spy, but not as you think, for the Germans, but for one of your Allies—the French."

The British sent Mata Hari back to Spain, where she had a romance with the German military attaché. He sent a coded message to Berlin indicating that spy "H-21" had been "valuable" even though he knew the Allies had cracked the code. In Paris, the exotic dancer was arrested and accused of selling secrets to the Germans. She admitted to taking money for love, but not for secrets. Although the evidence was scanty, Mata Hari was convicted and shot.

MATA HARI IN COSTUME AND LETTER WRITTEN BY MATA HARI

When Mata Hari was executed, the Allies were paranoid about spies. Some historians believe she was framed, and her death was meant to send a warning to anyone who was thinking of spying for the Germans. Others believe she was indeed a German spy.

A WOMAN CALLED MOSES
Harriet Tubman

"I GREW UP LIKE A NEGLECTED WEED," Harriet Tubman said, "ignorant of liberty, having no experience of it." By the age of six, she was a house servant on a plantation in Maryland, and by thirteen, bent over in the fields. In 1849, she escaped and followed the North Star. "When I found I had crossed the line [into the North]," she said, "I looked at my hands to see if I were the same person."

In Philadelphia, Harriet Tubman became a maid and a member of the Underground Railroad. The organization, run by ex-slaves and abolitionists, ran a network of safe houses and tunnels. Runaway slaves rode "the Railroad" to escape bondage. When she had enough money, Tubman slipped through the woods of Baltimore and helped members of her family escape. In the years prior to the Civil War, she made eighteen trips and freed three hundred slaves. On many of the trips, she was shot at. The state of Maryland nailed wanted posters to trees, offering $12,000 for the illiterate ex-slave, dead or alive. An association of Southern plantation owners threw in an additional $40,000.

Harriet Tubman

> In my opinion there are few captains, perhaps few colonels, who have done more for the colored race than our fearless and sagacious friend, Harriet.
>
> —*John Brown*

In 1859, the governor of Massachusetts sent Tubman to Beaufort, South Carolina, to be a teacher and nurse to the Gullah people of the Sea Islands. When the Civil War broke out, she organized an intelligence-gathering network of spies and scouts and led them behind the Confederate lines. Tubman's most famous mission was in July 1863 with Colonel James Montgomery. Accompanied by three hundred black soldiers, they disrupted supply lines and destroyed bridges and railroads along the Combahee River. They also freed 756 slaves. On the way to Beaufort, Tubman sang to the frightened runaways to calm their nerves.

Harriet Tubman believed she should be paid by the army for her spying and sabotage activities. She received $200 and used a portion to open a laundry so that black women could earn money washing uniforms. To support herself, Tubman sold root beer and baked goods. Years later, she received some money from the government, but not for her spying. After the death of her husband, she got a "widow's pension."

"I don't know when I was born, but I am pretty near ninety-five," Tubman said in 1913. At the time, she was living in the Harriet Tubman Home for Aged and Indigent Negroes, which she had founded. Hours before her death, she directed a prayer service and sang with her friends. She was buried with full military honors.

This is the only military command in American history wherein a woman, black or white, led the raid and under whose inspiration it was originated and conducted.

—*Union General Saxton's report on Colonel Montgomery's raid*

EDITH CAVELL

EDITH CAVELL was a small British nurse with upswept hair and gray eyes. When German troops marched into Belgium in 1914, she was the "school's matron" at the Berkendael Institute, a nurses' training school outside of Brussels. "I am needed more than ever," she said. From November 1914 until October 1915, she hid two hundred British, French, and Belgian soldiers and helped them escape. She also tucked information into her undergarments and carried it across Holland.

When Cavell was arrested, she admitted to having helped the Allied soldiers. The only document that incriminated her was a ragged postcard with a warm thank-you signed by one of the men. (She had sewn her diary into a cushion.) Edith Cavell was shot at dawn on October 12, 1915, in her nurse's uniform.

LITERARY SPIES

WHY WRITE? Most authors are fascinated by plots and subplots, human behavior, motivations, great characters, and stories with surprise endings. Espionage is filled with twists and turns, bizarre behavior, heroes, traitors, and dramatic stories with unpredictable endings. Writers put puzzles together. Intelligence analysts also face puzzles, though they seldom have all the pieces. It's not surprising that many authors have written about espionage, and some have been spies.

> **There is no sin but ignorance.**
>
> —*Christopher Marlowe*

CHRISTOPHER MARLOWE (1564–1593)

Christopher Marlowe was an exceptional playwright. When he was murdered at twenty-nine, he was far more successful than his contemporary, William Shakespeare. "Kit" Marlowe was also a spy for the Privy Council "in matters touching the benefit of his country." He probably worked for Sir Francis Walsingham, spymaster of Queen Elizabeth I. His murder (he was stabbed to death supposedly over a bar bill) may have been staged to keep him from revealing secrets about Walsingham's network.

SIR FRANCIS BACON (1561–1626)

Sir Francis Bacon, "the Father of Modern Science," was a scholar, writer, and a member of Queen Elizabeth's spy network. From 1580 to 1591, he gathered intelligence throughout Europe on the "laws, religion, military strength and whatsoever concerneth pleasure or profit" for the British monarch. In 1626, Bacon wanted to test freezing on the preservation of meat. He went outside in a blizzard and stuffed snow into a chicken. His theory was correct, but Bacon died of pneumonia a month later.

DANIEL DEFOE (1660–1731)

British author Daniel Defoe wrote over 370 books, including *Robinson Crusoe* and *Moll Flanders*. He also did intelligence work in exchange for getting out of prison. Both a spy and a spymaster of a vast network in the early 1700s, he had more than twenty pseudonyms.

> Every novelist has something in common with a spy; he watches, he overhears, he seeks motives and analyzes character.
>
> —*Graham Greene*

W. SOMERSET MAUGHAM (1874–1965)

W. Somerset Maugham was a novelist and playwright of Irish ancestry. During World War I he was an ambulance driver for the British Red Cross attached to the French Army. Later, he became a spy in Switzerland and then in Petrograd, Russia. (His job was to gather intelligence on the Russian Revolution.) He is sometimes credited with inventing the modern spy story.

GRAHAM GREENE (1904–1991)

British novelist, playwright, and poet Graham Greene spied briefly for the German government when he was in college. In 1940, he joined MI6. (His supervisor was Kim Philby of the Cambridge spies.) Greene's espionage activities in Sierra Leone, West Africa, inspired some of his twenty-six novels.

BEHIND CLOSED CURTAINS

IN TWELFTH-CENTURY JAPAN, professional spies were called ninjas. The word comes from *ninjitsu,* which means "the art of the shadow." Ninjas were trained to be invisible. Using "shadow skills," they gathered information and sabotaged their enemies without being detected. They dressed in dark uniforms at night, white in the snow, and camouflage in the forest. So what is the opposite of an invisible ninja, the least likely spy of all? A celebrity.

Imagine a celebrity in the middle of a covert operation surrounded by onlookers. "Aren't you so and so?" they ask. "Can I have your autograph?" Could a celebrity ever become unnoticeable? Perhaps not, but a few celebrities did spy. German movie star Marlene Dietrich used her celebrity status and sensuous voice to undermine the Nazis. Actor Sterling Hayden, director John Ford, and professional baseball player Moe Berg worked for the OSS. Sometimes famous people gain access simply because they're "stars." Many have performed well in the limelight, but also behind closed curtains.

> Everything shimmered in secrecy, and it was a rare man who knew what his fellows were doing.
>
> —*Sterling Hayden*

JOHN FORD (1895–1973)

Director John Ford sailed the South Seas in the late 1930s and reported on the activities of the Japanese Navy. After the war broke out, he became chief of the OSS Field Photographic Branch, a division of American intelligence that was responsible for aerial surveillance and mapping.

JOHN LE CARRÉ (1931–)

John le Carré (born David John Moore Cornwell) worked for both MI5 and MI6 (1959–1964). His intelligence work inspired his writing, and his third book, *The Spy Who Came In from the Cold*, became a best-seller and a movie.

MARLENE DIETRICH (1901–1992)

When World War II broke out, Hitler ordered the German movie star Marlene Dietrich to return to her homeland. Instead, she became a U.S. citizen. In 1944, Dietrich made radio broadcasts for the OSS. In her familiar, sultry voice, she sang and read nostalgic lyrics to the weary German troops. The propaganda was meant to lower morale and increase defections. Dietrich also entertained American troops on the front lines. After the war, she received the highest civilian honor from the U.S. government, the Medal of Freedom.

STERLING HAYDEN (1916–1986)

Actor Sterling Hayden, who some considered the most beautiful man in Hollywood, left the movies to fight in World War II. He enlisted in the Marines as John Hamilton, then joined the OSS. Hayden became an expert seaman, commanding a squadron of ships. The actor and his men provided guns and supplies to Yugoslavian guerrillas fighting the Nazis. After the war, Sterling Hayden starred in the movie *Dr. Strangelove*.

MOE BERG

AN EDITOR AT *THE NEW YORK TIMES* wrote an article mentioning Moe Berg and received a letter in the mail. It was signed by Moe Berg, but the ballplayer had been dead for years. Just before the museum curator at the CIA turns off the lights every night, she goes over to two baseball cards and says, "Good night, Moe." Berg was so unusual, it's easy to imagine that he's still listening.

At Princeton University, Moe Berg pursued two passions: languages and baseball. His classmates, mostly Christians from wealthy backgrounds, often discriminated against the Jewish son of Russian immigrants. On the baseball field, success depended not on your background, but on your skill. Moe Berg is still considered the "best baseball player in the school's history."

After college, Berg played for the Brooklyn Robins, the Minneapolis Millers, the Toledo Mud Hens, the Philadelphia Keystones, the Chicago White Sox, the Washington Senators, the Boston Red Sox, and the Cleveland Indians. While he was under contract, he got a law degree and passed the New York Bar. "Professor Berg" was considered "the brainiest man ever to have played the game," but he wasn't a star baseball player.

Berg dressed in a dark gray suit, white shirt, and black tie after the games, and went home to his newspapers and books. He could charm his teammates and the press with his knowledge and amusing stories, but no one really knew him. When asked why he wore the same dapper but colorless outfit every day (he had eight identical sets), he replied that he was "in mourning for the world." The ballplayer behaved like a man with secrets.

In 1934, Japan was openly hostile with the United States. The Japanese suspected that many camera-toting tourists were spies and limited their photography. On a baseball tour with Babe Ruth and Lou Gehrig, Berg ignored the warnings and slid his camera out from under his jacket. He also slipped away from one game, put on a kimono, and took an elevator up the tallest building in Tokyo. With a motorized camera, he filmed the entire city, including the harbor and military installations. (The films may have been used for the bombing of Tokyo.)

A month after the Japanese bombed Pearl Harbor, Berg left baseball and went to work for the Office of Inter-American Affairs (OIAA), and later, the OSS.

The greatest secret of World War II was the atomic bomb. Germany and the Allies knew that the first one to create the bomb would win the war. The OSS sent Berg to Italy to find out the location of the top German scientists, Werner Heisenberg and Carl Friedrich von Weizsacker, and the extent of their research. On May 4, 1944, Berg (code name: Remus) flew out of Washington, D.C., with a pistol in his pocket.

In Italy, Berg provided the OSS with valuable information on German radar, radio-guided bombs, and aerial torpedoes. When Heisenberg delivered a talk in Switzerland, Berg was in the audience. Reportedly, his orders were to shoot Heisenberg if the scientist appeared to know too much, and take an L-pill (suicide pill) if captured. Nothing in Heisenberg's lecture persuaded Berg to use the gun. Despite German propaganda to the contrary, Germany never had the bomb.

I love her [America] so tenderly that even her spots, her blemishes, are dear unto to me.

—*Moe Berg*

After the war, Berg was offered the Medal of Freedom, but he turned it down. He couldn't explain the medal, because his activities were classified, so it didn't interest him. He just wanted to be a spy. Berg participated in a few more operations for the OSS and CIA, but the agencies let him go. The ballplayer was too independent, too financially irresponsible, too unpredictable. He was brilliant and fearless, but he didn't follow the rules.

In the last third of his life, Berg hardly worked at all. When people asked him what he did, he often put his finger over his lips and said, "Shh." He showed up unannounced, departed suddenly, and sometimes hid behind a bush or a column. Berg lived with his brother for seventeen years (despite two eviction notices) and his sister for eight. The rest of the time he was an entertaining guest of friends and strangers.

At a World Series Boston Red Sox game in 1967, Berg was introduced to a doctor sitting in a box reserved for journalists. "I'm a phony, too," he said. It was an interesting remark from a man who wanted everyone to think he was a spy long after his career ended. Of course, spies are "phonies," but many are heroes, too.

IMAGINARY SPIES

WHAT IF SPYING WASN'T SECRET? If you could read every detail of CIA operations in Beijing or Baghdad in the morning newspaper, there would be no need to wonder. It's the secrecy that stimulates curiosity and the imagination. In Washington, D.C., there may be more spies than anyplace else on earth. What are they all doing? Writers and movie producers provide answers. The rest of us—the ones who are dying to know—stand in line at bookstores and theaters.

Most of the books and movies are inspired by reality. John le Carré's experiences working for the British foreign service inspired *The Spy Who Came In from the Cold.* "Not that it matters," Ian Fleming said about his book *From Russia with Love,* "but a great deal of the background to this story is accurate." Writers get material from intelligence agencies, and agencies sometimes get ideas from the writers and other artists.

In World War II, the military used the ideas of movie set designers to create the inflatables for the D-Day deception campaign. The CIA turned to John Chambers, the makeup artist from *Planet of the Apes* to help create disguises for the escape during the Iran hostage crisis. In the 1960s, KGB agents watched the television program *Mission: Impossible* because they were convinced that they would learn CIA techniques. At the same time, CIA officers were assigned to watch the show in case they were asked, "Can you guys do that?"

[CIA] teams have even been sent to pick the brains of Hollywood scriptwriters who dream up far-fetched terror spectaculars. . . . The CIA has found evidence in seized Al Qaeda documents that bin Laden's operatives watch action-adventure movies for ideas.

—Time *magazine*

One spy in the right place is worth 20,000 men in the field.

—*Napoleon*

ALIAS

Like OSS agent Virginia Hall, Sydney Bristow uses aliases and disguises to hide her real identity. In the television program *Alias*, Sydney is a CIA operative (code names: Freelancer, Mountaineer). She speaks thirteen languages and is adept at Krav Maga (the self-defense and hand-to-hand combat system of Israel) and electromagnetic lock picking.

GET SMART

Get Smart premiered in 1965. The Cold War produced the spy craze that inspired the television show. Maxwell Smart was a spoof of James Bond. The elegant Agent 007 used futuristic technology to outwit the enemy. The bumbling Maxwell Smart communicated on a shoe phone. His most familiar line began, "Would you believe . . ." (*Get Smart* ran for five seasons.)

A CIA AND A KGB

GENERAL OLEG DANILOVICH KALUGIN, CHIEF OF FOREIGN COUNTERINTELLIGENCE, KGB

OLEG KALUGIN was a correspondent for Radio Moscow, and a press secretary and public relations officer at the Soviet Embassy in Washington, D.C. At the same time, he was running several major spy networks, including the Walker spy ring. At age forty, Kalugin was brought back to Moscow and made chief of Foreign Counterintelligence at the KGB. His job was to "locate people who were guilty of high treason and provide information for the execution." The youngest general in the history of the KGB became an American citizen in 2003.

What is the biggest misconception about spying? Spying is a battle of wits, wills, and spirits. It's not just information collection. It's also acting according to the information to promote the foreign policy objectives of the country.

How does the KGB's approach differ from the CIA's? Russian agencies emphasize "human" intelligence penetration with agents inside the targeted countries. Here (in the U.S.) the emphasis has been largely on "signal" intelligence and collection through technical means.

What are the strengths or weaknesses of American intelligence? The U.S. has all the capabilities. It's a great nation, great money, great technology, everything at its disposal to lead the world, but for too long it neglected human intelligence.

Were you ever scared? I'm not easily scared. I did have anonymous threats from former colleagues and the current Russian security service. One of the letters talked about the beautiful cemeteries in the U.S. and they hoped that I'll find rest in one of them. But sometimes, they're far more rude.

Did you carry a weapon? We never carried weapons in our foreign assignments. Our weapons were our training, our intelligence, and our understanding of what was going on. We did use miniature recording devices and bugged the State Department, the Foreign Relations Committee, a major technology company doing business with the Defense Department, and U.S. embassies abroad.

What would you like young people to know about espionage? Kids should know that it's great work. The challenge is to turn your potential enemy into your friend. If you succeed, you're the right guy. It's not about driving fast cars like James Bond. You have to be knowledgeable, hardworking, imaginative, and have the ability to build bridges of understanding with other people, winning them over to your side. It's a very exciting, challenging job.

OFFICER TALK

SANDY GRIMES, INTELLIGENCE OFFICER, SOVIET/EAST EUROPEAN OPERATIONS, CENTRAL INTELLIGENCE AGENCY

SANDY GRIMES WAS A RUSSIAN MAJOR at the University of Washington. She signed up for an interview with a CIA recruiter because she wanted a job. After routine medical and security clearances, including a background check and polygraph test, Grimes joined the agency. For the next twenty-seven years (1967–1994), she worked in Soviet/East European Operations at CIA headquarters in Virginia, and during brief stints abroad in Africa, Europe, and Asia. (Soviet spy Aldrich Ames worked in the same division.)

Why do we need an intelligence agency? In order to protect yourself, you have to have both an offense and a defense—like a football game. You can't just defend yourself. You must get to know the enemy. At the CIA, we learn how the enemy thinks.

What was your job? I worked in Soviet Operations, where our responsibility was to recruit and run Soviet citizens, primarily government officials, who provided our government with Soviet state secrets [classified information]. In my case, I handled recruited sources who were Soviet intelligence officers [KGB and GRU]. We set up meetings with assets [spies], evaluated security risks, obtained equipment, put together questions, and coordinated follow-up. The assets were a huge responsibility. It was our job to make certain that they spied, they retired, and no one ever knew about them. It was serious work, because the assets' lives were at risk. The punishment for conviction of high treason in the Soviet Union was a bullet to the head and an unmarked grave.

Was there any difference in the way men and women approached the work? The approach to the work was identical. You had to be adventurous, understand human beings, and realize the world isn't black and white. The problem-solving is most frequently in shades of gray. It's like peeling an onion. What appears on the first layer is not the same as what's on the next layer down. When I arrived at the agency, there were lots of women, mostly in secretarial and clerical jobs. Now there are many women in high-level positions.

Were you ever scared? No. I tend not to be fearful.

How do you convince someone to spy? You'll never convince someone to spy unless they're predisposed to do it. You offer something that they want—to get back at their own system, money, or approval. The truth is that the best spies were all volunteers.

YOU SETTLE INTO YOUR CUSHY, LEATHER CHAIR and gaze out the window at the Virginia landscape. Behind you, thousands of people are devising "covers," protecting assets (spies), figuring out ways to gather intelligence, and analyzing secrets. You think back to the beginning. Was the first spy wrong? Should he have climbed a tree to steal secrets from his neighbor? You notice a hawk sitting high up in an enormous oak tree. He shifts his weight, but his eyes are locked on the ground. Somewhere there's a small animal who doesn't know he's being watched. The hawk has no doubts about his covert operations, but you, the head of Central Intelligence, must ask questions.

What if a foreign leader is brutalizing his own people or posing a threat to his neighbors or the United States? Is it proper for a government to affect a political change in another country? What if a suspected terrorist is hiding information that could save lives? Is it right to subject him to physical and mental abuse during an interrogation? Should a government spy on its suspicious citizens in a free country? Should a security agency keep track of who takes books on bomb-making out of a library? What about books on spying? The decisions will be made by others—the White House, Department of Justice, or another agency—but they will seek your opinion. What do you think?

Good intelligence doesn't guarantee good policy, but poor intelligence can ensure bad policy.

—*Congressman Lee H. Hamilton*

CIA Headquarters in Langley, Virginia

HEAD OF THE CIA

WE NEVER SLEEP

The Pinkerton agency logo. This all-seeing eye inspired the term "private eye."

You glance at a photo on the wall. It's a picture of the President of the United States in front of the Rose Garden. You're standing next to him, shaking his hand and grinning. You lean back in your oversized chair and consider the history of espionage. The stories of heroes, traitors, operations, and mistakes are reassuring, because your country has faced hideous threats and survived. You know that nations have to protect themselves, especially in a nuclear and biological-warfare age. The best way is to find out how the enemy thinks, and what they're planning. "We not only have to spy," you say even though no one is listening, "we have to outspy our foes." Then you remember George Washington, who beat the British by outspying them over two centuries ago.

You think about the wooden horse, onionskins with secret messages, pigeons with cameras, and dummy plywood airplanes. You try to imagine the ideas that will become fantastic operations or deceptions in the future, and the technology they will inspire. The tools are important, but the most valuable weapon is the human being—the people in the offices nearby and the spies risking their lives out in the field. You glance out the window. The hawk is gone.

BIBLIOGRAPHY

A Yankee Spy in Richmond: The Civil War Diary of "Crazy Bet" Van Lew, edited by David D. Ryan, Stackpole Books, 1996.

Confessions of a Spy: The Real Story of Aldrich Ames, Pete Earley, G. P. Putnam's Sons, 1997.

Family of Spies: Inside the John Walker Spy Ring, Pete Earley, Bantam Books, 1988.

Great Spy Stories, edited by Allen Dulles, Harper & Row, 1968.

Hidden Secrets: A Complete History of Espionage and the Technology Used to Support It, David Owen, Firefly Books Ltd., 2002.

In Disguise: Stories of Real Women Spies, Ryan Ann Hunter, Beyond Words Publishing, Inc., 2003.

Know It All: 5087 Weird and Wacky Trivia Questions and Answers, Marsha Kranes, Fred Worth, and Steve Temerius, Tess Press, 1998.

Operatives, Spies, and Saboteurs: The Unknown Story of the Men and Women of WW II's OSS, Patrick K. O'Donnell, Free Press, 2004.

Saboteurs: The Nazi Raid on America, Michael Dobbs, Alfred A. Knopf, New York, 2004.

Sisterhood of Spies: The Women of the OSS, Elizabeth P. McIntosh, G.K. Hall & Co., 1998.

Spies Beneath Berlin, David Stafford, The Overlook Press, 2002.

Spies for the Blue and Gray, Harnett Thomas Kane, Hanover House, 1954.

Spy Book: The Encyclopedia of Espionage, 2nd Edition, Norman Polmar and Thombas B. Allen, Random House Reference, 2004.

Spies: The Undercover World of Secrets, Gadgets and Lies, David Owen, Quintet Publishing, Ltd., 2003.

Spy Hunter: Inside the FBI Investigation of the Walker Espionage Case, Robert W. Hunter, Naval Institute Press, 1999.

Spy Stories, U.S. News and World Report, Inc., 2003.

Spying: The Secret History of History, Black Dog and Leventhal Publishers, 2004.

Sun-Tzu: The Art of Warfare: The First English Translation Incorporating the Recently Discovered Yin-ch'ueh-shan Texts, Roger Ames, Ballantine Books, 1993.

The Catcher Was a Spy, The Mysterious Life of Moe Berg, Nicholas Dawidoff, Vintage Books, 1994.

The Code Book: The Evolution of Secrecy from Mary Queen of Scots to Quantum Cryptography, Simon Singh, Anchor, 2000.

The Literary Spy, Charles E. Lathrop, Yale University Press, 2004.

The Memoirs of Jacques Casanova, Giacomo Casanova, edited by Madeleine Boyd, Modern Library, 1957.

The Spy Who Saved the World: How a Soviet Colonel Changed the Course of the Cold War, Jerrold L. Schecter and Peter S. Deriabin, Scribner, 1992.

The White Rabbit, Bruce Marshall, The Riverside Press, 1952.

The Wizards of Langley, Jeffrey T. Richelson, Westview Press, 2001.

Theremin: Ether Music and Espionage, Albert Glinsky, University of Illinois Press, 2000.

Ultimate Spy, H. Keith Melton, Dorling Kindersley Inc., 2002.

Web Sites
www.americancivilwar.com
www.atomicmuseum.com
www.eh.doe.gov
www.jewishvirtuallibrary.org
www.seferad.org
www.thebiographychannel.com

Articles
"The Spy Who Changed History," Chitra Ragavan (Larry Wu Tai Chin) *U.S. News & World Report,* www.chitraravagan.com.

ILLUSTRATION CREDITS

2MPOD —J. W. C.

With my thanks to tireless and talented editor Tamar Brazis at Harry N. Abrams, Inc.,
and Peter Earnest and Thomas Boghardt at the International Spy Museum.

Design by Celina Carvalho
Production Manager: Alexis Mentor

Library of Congress Cataloging-in-Publication Data

Coleman, Janet Wyman.
Secrets, lies, gizmos, and spies : a history of spies and espionage / by Janet Wyman Coleman.
p. cm.
Published in association with the International Spy Museum.
1. Intelligence service—History. 2. Espionage—History. I. International Spy Museum (Washington, D.C.) II. Title.

UB250.C59 2006
327.12009—dc22
2005027824

Principal Consultants: Peter Earnest, Executive Director, International Spy Museum,
and Dr. Thomas Boghardt, Historian, International Spy Museum

With special thanks to Milt and Tamar Maltz, Joan G. Stanley of J. G. Stanley & Co., Inc.

Printed and bound in China
10 9 8 7 6 5 4 3 2 1

HNA
harry n. abrams, inc.
a subsidiary of La Martinière Groupe
115 West 18th Street
New York, NY 10011
www.hnabooks.com

Visit the International Spy Museum, 800 F Street NW, Washington, D.C., 20004, and spymuseum.org